OSPREY COMBAT AIRCRAFT • 71

Il-2 *SHTURMOVIK*
GUARDS UNITS
OF WORLD WAR 2

SERIES EDITOR: TONY HOLMES

OSPREY COMBAT AIRCRAFT • 71

Il-2 *SHTURMOVIK* GUARDS UNITS OF WORLD WAR 2

OLEG RASTRENIN

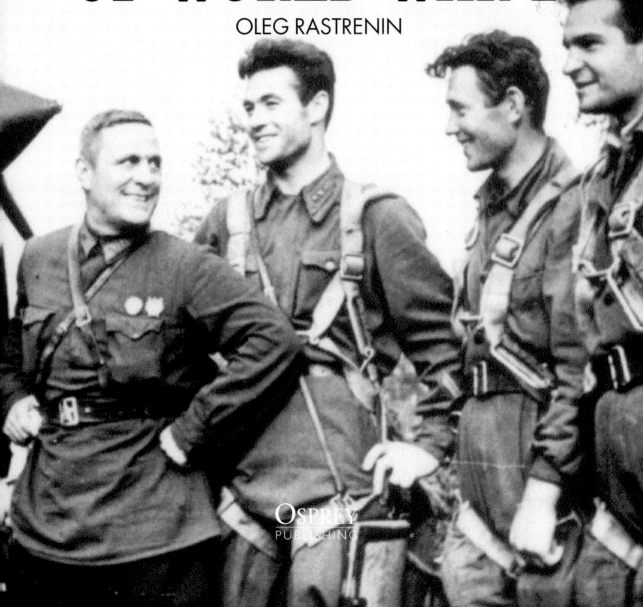

OSPREY
PUBLISHING

Front cover
Jnr Lt V P Aleksukhin and air gunner
A D Gatayunov attack German
armoured targets on the Kharkhov
sector of the front during the epic
Battle of Kursk in August 1943.
Acknowledged as being the best
flight crew in 617th ShAP (167th
GShAP from February 1944),
V P Aleksukhin and A D Gatayunov
routinely flew this uniquely marked
Il-2 as they hunted down enemy
troop trains and armour. The aircraft
bore the inscription *Aleksandr
Suvorov* on its fuselage, and also
boasted a likeness of the famous
Russian field marshal on its tail
too – dubbed the 'Eagle of the Alps',
Suvorov had led the Austro-Russian
forces that defeated the armies
of the French Republic in Italy in
1798-99. One of the great generals
of modern times, Suvorov was never
defeated in battle. He ascribed his
success to the principle of 'intuition,
rapidity, impact', and V P Aleksukhin
and A D Gatayunov did their best to
stick to emulate these attributes
during the 40+ sorties that they flew
in August 1943 *(Cover artwork by
Mark Postlethwaite)*

First published in Great Britain in 2008 by Osprey Publishing
Midland House, West Way, Botley, Oxford, OX2 0PH
443 Park Avenue South, New York, NY, 10016, USA
E-mail; info@ospreypublishing.com

ISBN 13: 978 1 84603 296 7

Edited by Bruce Hales-Dutton and Tony Holmes
Page design by Tony Truscott
Cover Artwork by Mark Postlethwaite
Aircraft Profiles and Scale Drawings by Andrey Yurgenson
Indexed by Alan Thatcher
Originated by PDQ Digital Media Solutions
Printed in China through Bookbuilders

08 09 10 11 12   10 9 8 7 6 5 4 3 2 1

For a catalogue of all books published by Osprey please contact:
NORTH AMERICA
Osprey Direct, c/o Random House Distribution Center, 400 Hahn Road,
Westminster, MD 21157. E-mail: info@ospreydirect.com

ALL OTHER REGIONS
Osprey Direct UK, P.O. Box 140 Wellingborough, Northants, NN8 2FA, UK.
E-mail: info@ospreydirect.co.uk
(www.ospreypublishing.com)

ACKNOWLEDGEMENTS
The Author would like to extend his sincere appreciation to the countless
individuals that helped him during the preparation of this book, and also to
the following former Il–2 pilots for their feats of arms – Twice Hero of the
Soviet Union Marshal of Aviation A N Evimov, Hero of the Soviet Union
Gen-Maj of Aviation V A Kumskov, Hero of the Soviet Union Col B N Levin,
full holder of the Order of Glory Capt G A Litvin and Hero of the Soviet
Union Col V K Tikhonenko.

PHOTOGRAPHIC SOURCES
The photographs in this book have been sourced from the Central Archive of
the Ministry of Defence of Russia, the Russian State Archive of Cinema and
Photo Documents, the Museum of Aviation and Cosmonautics of Samara State
Aviation University, the archives of G F Petrov and A Drabkin and, finally,
the Author.

CONTENTS

INTRODUCTION

By order of the USSR People's Commissar of Defence, dated 6 December 1941, six air regiments that had distinguished themselves defending Moscow and Leningrad were awarded the title of Guards units. They were 29th IAP (*Istrebitelniy Aviatsionniy Polk – Fighter Air Regiment*), 129th IAP, 526th IAP, 155th IAP, 31st BAP (*Bombardirovochniy Aviatsionniy Polk – Bomber Air Regiment*) and 215th ShAP (*Shturmovoy Aviatsionniy Polk – Attack Air Regiment*). They were the first aviation units to receive the coveted Guards title.

The attack regiments represented the major strike force of VVS RKKA (*Voenno-Vozdushnye Sily Raboche-Krestiyanskoy Krasnoy Armii – Air Force of the Workers' and Peasants' Red Army*) throughout World War 2. Yet despite their efforts in combat, the subject of Guards attack aviation units, and their contribution to the defeat of Nazi Germany, has yet to receive appropriate coverage in the literature of military history.

VVS RKKA trained and sent to the front a total of 356 attack aircraft regiments, as well as forming 48 attack aircraft divisions and ten attack aircraft corps. From these, 48 air regiments, 12 air divisions and three air corps were designated as Guards units due to their exploits in combat.

Such units received special Guards banners, and following an order from the People's Commissar of Defence, dated 28 May 1942, Guards ranks and a *Gvardiya* (Guards) breast badge were also introduced. A further order, issued on 4 May 1943, required that personnel transferring in and out of Guards units could only do so with the permission of VVS RKKA's commanding officer. Units receiving the Guards title also had to be at full strength all the time.

Apart from the prestige associated with being in a Guards unit, personnel also enjoyed financial rewards. The pay for commanding officers was one-and-a-half times better than that enjoyed by the COs of regular air regiments, and for flight crews it was twice as high.

At first, Guards fighter and attack aircraft regiments were numbered separately, but from November 1942 numbers were allocated irrespective of their combat arm. Attack aircraft divisions and corps were numbered in the order in which they received the Guards title. When an air division was transformed into a Guards unit, it was initially assumed that all the air regiments within it would take that title as well. The same held true for the divisions and regiments of a Guards air corps. Later, however, such formations could include both Guards and non-Guards units.

The awarding of the title depended on an evaluation of the unit's combat record by its superior officers, as well as the quality of its personnel, and their organisation. The opinion of party bosses and political commissars was also crucial, and the title was not lightly bestowed. For example, 61st ShAP did not become 165th GShAP until 4 February 1944, yet it had fought from the very outbreak of war, been awarded the Order of the Red Banner in December 1941 and made a significant contribution to the development of attack aircraft tactics.

The reason for the unit being denied Guards status for so long can be traced back to late October 1941, when the regiment had been unable to carry out a combat mission assigned to it. 61st ShAP CO, Lt Col Mamushkin, and the regimental military commissar, Senior Political Officer Miroshkin, were both reprimanded by 47th SAD (*Smeshannaya Aviatsionniy Diviziya* – Combined Air Division) CO, Col Tolstikov, for what he called 'poor organisation of and control over aircraft and armament preparations for a combat mission'.

This was by no means uncommon. 1st ShAK (*Shturmovoy Aviatsionniy Korpus* – Attack Aviation Corps), 291st ShAD (*Shturmovoy Aviatsionniy Diviziya* – Attack Air Division) and 299th ShAD were all due to have become Guards units for their valour in the Battle of Kursk in August 1943, but during the bitter fighting they had inadvertently attacked friendly troops. It took them a long time to prove their right to the Guards title. In several other cases, orders for particular units to receive the Guards title were drawn up but not signed for similar reasons. As a result, there are gaps in the numbering of Guards units. This is why there are no 13th or 14th Guards attack aircraft divisions, for example.

At the same time, when 2nd Guards Night Bomber Air Division was transformed into an attack aircraft division (by order of the People's Commissar of Defence, dated 17 September 1944), it retained its Guards title and received the number 15. 12th Guards Attack Aircraft Division was upgraded almost a month later.

The lack of a Guards title should not diminish the standing of other units, or their personnel, however. Members of Guards and non-Guards units both fought and died in the same fierce battles. On the other hand, bestowing the honorary title of 'guardsman' and Guards units raised morale, and may well have hastened victory over an able and battle-hardened enemy.

DEVELOPMENT OF THE Il-2

The mount of numerous Guards units, the Ilyushin Il-2 fully deserves its place in history. Not only was it built in larger numbers than any other combat aircraft in World War 2, but to the people of the Soviet Union it represented a symbol of their resistance to Nazi aggression. As a

This series production Il-2 AM-38 was photographed in the spring of 1942 shortly after being rolled off the production line at Zavod (Factory) No 18 in Voronezh. The single-seat aircraft is armed with two VYa-23 23 mm cannon, and it also boasts four rocket rails under each wing

A two-seat Il-2 AM-38 with a rear-facing 12.7 mm UBT machine gun undergoes state flight trials in October 1942. This particular aircraft was built by Factory No 30

specialised ground attack aircraft, with armour protection for the crew and vital systems, it was one of the conflict's most decisive weapons.

Yet the Il-2 was not a highly sophisticated machine. In fact, with its mixed wood and metal construction, it was comparatively crude, but this made it easy to produce using relatively unskilled labour. Outstandingly robust, it could absorb considerable battle damage, but although undemanding to fly, it was not a nimble performer, and was consequently highly vulnerable to fighter attack in the early war years.

In the late 1930s, the Soviets were placing much emphasis on ground attack aircraft. While experience in Spain and China had confirmed their effectiveness, it had also demonstrated that such aircraft needed protection against ground fire. In January 1938, Ilyushin and his team put forward ideas for a dedicated attack aircraft. Designated TsKB-55, it was a two-seater powered by a supercharged AM-35 engine, with the crew, fuel and oil systems protected by armour plate varying in thickness from 4 mm up to 8 mm. Four 100-kg bombs could be carried in internal bays, with an additional pair hung from underwing racks.

The design was accepted and two prototypes were ordered, the first making its maiden flight on 2 October 1939 and the second following on 30 December. During State acceptance trials, the aircraft was found to be underpowered, but with the fitment of the specially-developed low altitude unsupercharged AM-38 engine, and the deletion of the gunner's position, test pilots reported a major improvement in performance.

Fixed armament comprised two 23 mm PTB-23 cannon and two 7.62 mm SkHAS machine guns, with eight launching rails for rocket projectiles fitted beneath the wing outer panels. In this form the aircraft was cleared for service, and the first production Il-2 was completed by Zavod No 18 at Voronezh. It flew for the first time on 10 March 1941, just three months after the drawings had been delivered to the factory.

Although in full-scale production by the time of the German invasion on 22 June 1941, only 70 of the 249 Il-2s built up to then were actually in service. Production increased rapidly, however, and during the second half of 1941, 1293 left various factories in the USSR.

The first offensive mission mounted by a *Shturmovik* unit was flown on 1 July during the fighting around the city of Bobruysk and along the Berezina river. Heavy losses were inflicted by German fighter pilots during these operations, the *Jagdwaffe* units having quickly discovered the Il-2's blind spots. Soviet ground attack units in turn called on Ilyushin to build a two-seat variant with a gunner operating a flexibly-mounted 12.7 mm BT machine gun. This version started rolling off the assembly lines in 1942, and some earlier single-seat machines were also converted.

By 1943 one-third of all Soviet-built combat aircraft in frontline service were Il-2s. When production ended in November 1944, 36,163 *Shturmoviks* had been built.

STRIKE FORCE DEVELOPMENT

Before the Great Patriotic War, as World War 2 is still known in Russia, attack aviation was considered to be the spearhead of the Red Army, providing close air support to ground troops. According to the Red Army Field Manual (draft of 1940), attack aviation was intended to 'provide air support to friendly ground forces, deliver air strikes against enemy tank formations and motorised convoys, destroy the enemy on the battlefield, in its staging areas and on the move, and attack enemy airfields, HQs, command and control posts, transport, defensive installations, bridges, crossing points and rail facilities'.

Combat tactics for close air support aircraft envisaged two primary methods of attack. These were from level flight at a minimum altitude of 150 m (500 ft) and from a zoom at small glide angles after a low-level run-in. Bombs carried by these aircraft would be fitted with delay fuses.

Attack air regiments were equipped with obsolete Polikarpov I-15bis and I-153 biplane fighters modified to carry bombs and rocket projectiles for low-level and dive attack missions. The armoured Il-2 (two-seat AM-38 variant) was the first purpose-designed attack aircraft to serve with VVS RKKA, having entered production in March 1941. Its combat capabilities were vastly superior to those of the modified biplane fighters.

The Il-2 was central to VVS RKKA's rearmament plans, with 11 attack aircraft regiments scheduled to be equipped with *Shturmoviks* within five frontline military districts by the end of 1941. Six other regiments deployed further from the front, and in the far eastern regions of the USSR, were to convert to the Il-2 by mid-1942. In addition, eight short-range bomber regiments were to also have re-equipped with the type by early 1942.

As of 22 June 1941, when Germany attacked the USSR, VVS RKKA attack aviation in the five military districts facing the invaders were operating 207 I-15bis and 193 I-153 fighters. These formations had received just 20 Il-2s by the time war broke out, five having been delivered to the Baltic Special Military District, eight to the Western Special Military District, five to the Caucasus Special Military District and two to the Odessa Military District. But not one had been included in the duty rosters of the units in what was soon to become the frontline. This was due to a lack of trained pilots.

4th BBAP (*Blizhnebombardirovochniy Aviatsionniy Polk –*

Series production Il-2 AM-38 construction number 381355, armed with two 20 mm ShVAK cannon, was manufactured by Factory No 381 in the spring of 1942

Short-Range Bomber Air Regiment) of the Kharkov Military District was the only unit to have modern attack aircraft on strength on 22 June, having received 63 Il-2s, but its pilots had not yet fully converted onto the type. According to official sources, 60 pilots and 102 engineers had been trained to operate and maintain the Il-2 by 22

June, but none had returned to their frontline units by that fateful date.

And even if they had reached 4th BBAP prior to the German invasion, pilots had not received any instruction in Il-2 combat tactics since there was no manual to study! Pre-war tactics were totally unsuited to the Il-2, and did not exploit its capabilities to their fullest extent.

The fact was that the People's Commissar of Defence had only signed the order for Il-2 combat tests on 31 May 1941. NII VVS (*Nauchno-Ispitatelniy Institut Voenno-Vozdushnykh Sil*– Air Force Scientific Testing Institute) issued the corresponding order on 20 June. By decree of the People's Commissar of Defence, dated 17 May 1941, independent flight crews and flights of the Caucasus Special Military District were to complete Il-2 service testing by 15 July 1941.

In actuality, tactics for the *Shturmovik* had to be worked out in the crucible of war in the first year of the conflict in the east, with regiments bearing heavy losses in both pilots and aircraft during this period.

With all frontline Il-2 units attached to combined services armies, combined air divisions and reserve and attack air groups of the Supreme High Command General Headquarters, Air Force command was totally unable to manoeuvre its forces efficiently and focus its main efforts on the primary German lines of advance.

In the early months of the war, Il-2s operated in groups of three to five aircraft, with *Shturmoviks* attacking their targets one at a time from a minimum altitude of 20-25 m (65-80 ft) up to 150-200 m (500-650 ft), using all their weapons in a single run over the target. Whatever the height at which they started their attack, pilots would always fire their guns and drop their bombs from low level. In the absence of enemy fighters or strong anti-aircraft defences, pilots would make two to three attack runs. When operating at low level, Il-2 pilots could capitalise on the element of

A rare in-flight view of a first series Il-2 over the Soviet Western Front in August 1941. The single-seat variant quickly proved to be highly vulnerable to German fighters, as navigator Capt E Koval of 243rd ShAP (later 78th GShAP) explained to Josef Stalin in a letter that he wrote to the Soviet premier in late 1942;

'I consider it my duty to request that the designer and the aircraft industry improve our formidable attack aircraft. The main shortcoming of the aircraft is that it is absolutely unprotected against hostile fighters attacking from behind. In most cases the fighter approaches from behind at 10 to 15 m (32 to 50 ft) and opens fire, trying to damage the engine or kill the pilot. Compensating for this shortcoming by providing fighter protection does not seem to be effective. Attack aircraft operate at low to extremely low altitudes, while escorting fighters have to fly at 1000 to 1500 m (3300 to 5000 ft) over the target. A rear gunner, therefore, is a necessity'

A sight feared by the *Wehrmacht* – a flight of Il-2s race over the battlefield during a low-level attack in the autumn of 1941

surprise to evade enemy fighters. Should they be intercepted close to the ground, invariably there was no room for effective combat manoeuvring by the attacking fighters.

Low-level attacks were problematic for the Il-2 pilots as well, however, as they found navigating to and from the target area no easy proposition. The short time they spent over the latter also made it difficult for commanders to coordinate their individual attack runs effectively. Combat experience, and follow-up firing-range tests, demonstrated that low-level operations did not allow the Il-2 to capitalise on its capabilities. The fact was that such tactics were the wrong ones, and could only be justified by the small number of Il-2s then in service, and the poor organisation of escorting fighter units. Western Front Air Force headquarters put it this way in a directive dated 8 August 1941;

'Il-2 attack aircraft suffer especially inept employment. Il-2 pilots are afraid of being shot down, and often unreasonably resort to low-level flight and lose their bearings, with the result that their missions fail.'

From August, therefore, in an effort to improve the effectiveness of attacks on small targets, groups of Il-2s were led by a mission controller in a Sukhoi Su-2, a Petlyakov Pe-2 or a fighter. They would designate the target by dropping bombs or AZh-2 incendiary spheres on it.

The following month, 66th ShAP of the Reserve Front Air Force started using a tactic developed by its CO, Col Shcheglikov. This called for the Il-2s to make diving attacks from an altitude of 600-1000 m (2000-3000 ft). This increased accuracy, but losses to anti-aircraft artillery rose. As a result, Gen Nikolaenko, Reserve Front Air Force CO, strictly prohibited operations at medium altitudes. Shcheglikov protested and was punished, his crime, according to Nikolaenko's directive of 14 August 1941, being 'the failure to comply with my personal directives that Il-2s are to operate at altitudes of up to 200-300 m. The

Old and new – a German horse-drawn convoy is attacked by Il-2s during the early weeks of the Great Patriotic War. Both sides made considerable use of horses throughout the conflict

commanding officer of the 66th ShAP, Col Shcheglikov, is hereby reprimanded, and warned about his incompetence'.

Accordingly, the correct method of using the Il-2, and of realising its effectiveness, remained unknown to Red Army attack aircraft flight crews until the spring of 1942.

On 7 August 1941 the State Defence Committee decided that each attack aircraft regiment was to comprise three squadrons and be equipped with 33 aircraft in total. This organisational structure was revised, however, after heavy losses, and the difficulties experienced in returning regiments to full strength. On 20 August the People's Commissar decreed that attack regiments were to include two units with nine aircraft each, plus two more aircraft assigned to the regimental headquarters.

During this period of heavy losses and general confusion, it was not uncommon for an entire regiment of 20 Il-2s to be thrown into action escorted by just one or two fighters. When the *Shturmoviks* were threatened by enemy fighters, often the only tactic employed by their escorts was to try and outrun the German Bf 109s, rather than attempting to engage them and provide their charges with mutual support. Under these circumstances, to say nothing of the superiority of German fighters and the experience of their pilots, it was hardly surprising that Il-2 units suffered heavy losses. In the early stages of the war, one Il-2 was lost on average for every eight to nine combat sorties.

NEW COMBAT TACTICS

Better tactics, which doubled Il-2 combat efficiency, were not developed until June-July 1942 after NIPAV (*Nauchno-Ispytatelniy Poligon Aviatsionnogo Vooruzheniya* – Aviation Armament Scientific Testing Firing Range) had conducted comprehensive tests on the aircraft's armament. Airborne firing trials proved that the Il-2 had to attack a small target like a tank or a lorry in a steep glide at an angle of 25-30 degrees from an altitude of 500-700 m (1600-2300 ft).

Typically, at least three runs over the target area were required to inflict significant damage. This meant that in the first, the Il-2 might launch four rockets at a range of 300-400 m (1000-1300 ft), in the second one it might drop its bombs while recovering from a dive and in the third it would strafe the target from a range of not more than 300-400 m.

Attacks against targets such as columns of infantry or convoys of vehicles were best carried out from low-level, or in a gentle 10-15-degree glide from an altitude of 100-200 m (300-650 ft), with bombs released in the second run. The essential condition was that the Il-2 had to use each type of armament separately.

Il-2s from 217th ShAP taxi out at the start of yet another combat mission on the Bryansk Front in August 1941

A lone Il-2 delivers a precise air strike somewhere over the Soviet steppe. During the early months of the war, the *Shturmovik* would typically carry just 200 kg (440 lb) of bombs. However, in mid-1942 The People's Commissariat of Defence ordered that a minimum bomb load of 400 kg (881 lb) had to be carried on combat missions, and crews routinely boosted this figure to 600 kg (1322 lb) as the war progressed

The 'closed loop', comprising at least six to eight Il-2s, was found to be the most effective combat formation because it facilitated defence-suppression and protection against enemy fighters. Targets were attacked in a dive from medium altitudes, with the 'closed loop' formation giving each aircraft enough space to both deliver precise bomb strikes and engage the target with accurate fire. It also enabled each member of the formation to shoot at enemy fighters attacking the Il-2 ahead.

Later, the 'loose circle' formation was adopted. This was indeed a circle, with varying distances between each aircraft that provided enough room for them to roll to either side. Otherwise, pilots were allowed total freedom of action. Despite the advantages, this formation failed to enable Il-2s recovering from their attacking dives to receive fire support, as the aircraft flying behind was too busy attacking the target. This meant that flak and fighter defences could concentrate on the Il-2s as they recovered from their attack runs. As a result, *Shturmovik* 'loose circle' formations included a special group of at least two to four aircraft to suppress air defences during the strike.

When operating altitudes were increased, Luftwaffe fighters started posing a real threat, as it was virtually impossible for Il-2s to operate at medium altitudes without fighter escort. When a formation withdrew from the target, stragglers were usually shot down. Even escorting fighters found it difficult to protect strung-out formations of Il-2s. Luftwaffe fighter attacks accounted for about 60 per cent of all Soviet attack aircraft losses during 1941-42. To the most aggressive Il-2 pilots there was only one answer – engage the enemy fighters.

Demonstration dogfights with various fighter types – Soviet Yak-7bs and Yak-1s and captured Bf 109E/Fs – proved that the Il-2 could out-turn these aircraft, even if the Ilyushin was less agile in a full turn. If the Il-2 decelerated sharply, a Messerschmitt attacking from behind would always overshoot and be vulnerable to the *Shturmovik's* guns.

'Scissors' manoeuvres were also found to be an effective way for a group of Il-2s to counter enemy fighters. By side-slipping with a 20-degree bank, pilots could prevent opposing fighters getting the Soviet attack aircraft into their sights. A flattened 'V'-shaped formation was also

A pair of Il-2s armed with RS-82 unguided rocket projectiles have their engines run up prior to take-off. The pilot of the aircraft closest to the camera is receiving last-minute instructions from a member of his groundcrew

considered effective for a group of six to eight Il-2s. While flying in pairs, they were to maintain a distance of 100-150 m between aircraft.

It was also recommended that Il-2s should repulse enemy fighters over hostile territory through a combination of head-on attacks and level manoeuvres, while still maintaining the general formation and direction of flight. Over friendly territory, forming a defensive circle was the best tactic, and this meant that Il-2 pilots would always turn towards the enemy when assuming their places in the circle. At the same time, the inside pairs would turn, dropping behind each other, while the outside pairs or wingmen stayed beside their leaders until the circle was closed.

It took at least six Il-2s to form an efficient circle, with aircraft spaced 150-200 m apart at an altitude of at least 300 m and banks at 15-40 degrees. In countering fighter attacks, Il-2 crews were to manoeuvre on the level, with bank angles of up to 45 degrees, pitching up and down up to 30 degrees.

The evolution of such tactics, and recommendations from aircrew in the frontline, played their part in reducing losses. But even more effective were the efforts of VVS KA commanding officers in making their pilots understand the Il-2's combat ability, and thus instilling self-confidence.

There are several examples of successful dogfights involving Il-2s, including one on 5 February 1943, when, because of a shortage of fighters, a group of Il-2s from 299th ShAD was briefed to defend Soviet ground troops against German bombing attacks near Livna. As the Il-2s withdrew, Lt Kalchik dropped behind the main formation and was attacked by a Bf 109. As the Messerschmitt overshot at high speed, Kalchik throttled back and banked to starboard. The enemy fighter duly flew past and Kalchik manoeuvred into position behind it. He fired his cannon and the Bf 109 burst into flame and crashed.

The Il-2 was then attacked by another Messerschmitt, and when it closed in, Kalchik banked to port and this Bf 109 also overshot. It literally disintegrated after another well-aimed burst of cannon fire. This battle was seen by 15th Air Army CO, Gen Pyatykhin, who after the dogfight, sent the following message to Col Krupskiy, CO of 299th ShAD;

'The attack aircraft pilot, who shot down two Me 109s in a dogfight near Livna is decorated with the Order of the Red Banner for the valour he displayed. Report the last name of the hero.'

Accordingly, Kalchik received his decoration that same night.

Capt Efimov – twice Hero of the Soviet Union (HSU), and a future air marshal – achieved the highest score of any Soviet attack aircraft pilot against German fighters. He carried out 285 combat sorties, engaged German fighters 53 times and is officially credited with seven aerial kills. He even conducted successful single-handed engagements against as many as eight fighters. In doing so, Efimov flew the Il-2 to the limit of its capabilities, drawing the enemy fighters down to lower altitudes, where they could not capitalise on their superior speed and manoeuvrability.

IMPROVED ORGANISATIONAL STRUCTURE

As combat tactics were being developed, so too was an improved Red Army Air Force organisational structure, together with better command and control. VVS authorities established air armies and air corps, and transformed mixed combined air divisions into uniform ones. An attack aircraft division now comprised three regiments, each equipped with 32 aircraft – three squadrons of ten Il-2s each, plus two aircraft attached to regimental headquarters.

But the new organisational structure still failed to meet wartime requirements, as ten-strong squadrons were exhausted by losses by the third or fourth day of combat operations. Due to serviceability and combat losses, it was also found that squadrons could rarely send more than six aircraft out on a mission at once, preventing them from countering anti-aircraft and fighter defences. Squadron strength was therefore raised to 14 Il-2s, with regimental strength brought up to 45. Squadrons would now be able to operate in groups of eight. The pair assigned to regimental headquarters constituted a reserve, which allowed combat formations to be tailored to the mission and the environment.

It was not until 1944 that Il-2 losses had been reduced sufficiently enough to allow VVS KA to embrace a 40-aircraft structure for all of its attack aircraft regiments.

The high demand for attack aircraft at the front resulted in little time for the training of pilots prior to them flying combat missions. On average, no more than 30 per cent of air crew assigned to a typical attack aircraft regiment had some previous combat experience. The remaining flight personnel had not only never heard a shot fired in anger, but had also logged little flying time in an Il-2. As a result, there were heavy losses, particularly amongst novice pilots. During the spring and summer of 1942, one Il-2 was lost for every 24 combat sorties, and in the Battle of Stalingrad the ratio increased to one aircraft per 10-12 combat sorties.

In the summer of 1943, Il-2 losses to enemy fighters began decreasing, although those to flak started to rise, which effectively kept the loss rate static. An analysis of attack aircraft losses during the Battle of Kursk shows that 49 per cent of all Il-2s shot down fell to anti-aircraft fire, with enemy fighters accounting for 37 per cent and the remaining 14 per cent being listed as 'missing in action' and 'other causes', the latter including bad weather and mechanical failures. Reports from a number of air armies during this period painted an even gloomier picture, with individual Il-2 units losing 60-65 per cent of their aircraft to anti-aircraft fire.

According to the VVS KA Air Gunnery Service Directorate, an Il-2 attacking a ground target within a German defensive area faced a hail of 8000-9000 large-calibre rounds and 200-300 small-calibre bullets every second. Given the fact that Il-2 formations wheeled over the battlefield at an altitude of 200-1000 m (650-3250 ft) for an average of ten to twenty minutes, heavy losses to flak were inevitable.

Another factor influencing the rate-of-loss to Luftwaffe fighters was that the average flying time logged by reserve unit attack aircraft pilots at least doubled during the second half of the war. The rule that flight crews were not sent to the front

Il-2s destroyed this *Sturmgeschütz III Ausf F* assault gun during an attack in 1943. Large numbers of these tank destroyers were employed by the Germans during their operations in the USSR, and they were routinely targeted by Il-2s

This photograph gives a good impression of the destructive power of the ROFS-132 high-explosive rocket projectile – a weapon widely employed by the Il-2. The Germans used considerable numbers of captured Czech-built tanks like this PzKpfw 38(t) Ausf S, and they proved to be no match for a well-aimed rocket projectile

The underwing-mounted ROFS-132 high-explosive rocket projectile was an extremely effective weapon when used against German military and transport targets

without proper combat training as a group – in pairs, as a flight or in squadron strength – was strictly applied. In addition, cooperation between Il-2s and escort fighters had reached a high level of effectiveness, as had the defensive tactics that were now being employed.

At the same time the strength of German frontline fighter units was now beginning to drastically decrease, and the quality of pilot training for replacement crews had deteriorated significantly. Their combat experience was no longer sufficient to enable them to conduct successful dogfights with what were by now seasoned Soviet pilots.

By the summer of 1943, there had also been considerable changes made to the Il-2 battlefield-based command and control system, which in turn facilitated closer cooperation with friendly ground forces. Forward ground-based spotters, now located in tanks and jeeps, operated as part of combat formations, while attack aircraft unit commanders remained at their command posts to facilitate liaison with friendly ground forces and speed up decision-making.

A direction centre was also established near the command post, and it was usually headed up by a resolute and determined commander with a high standard of tactical training and combat experience to his credit. This centre guided Il-2s to their targets, briefed pilots on local conditions, relayed orders from the air army commander and received reconnaissance and intelligence reports. Spotters embedded within joint combat formations were able to pinpoint the FLOT (Forward Line of Own Troops), and radio target information to Il-2 crews. From mid-1944, all frontline command and control sections operated like clockwork without failure or error. Their work resulted in considerable successes.

Il-2 combat tactics were honed during the war's final stage when enemy ground defences were significantly stepped-up. The number of fortifications doubled or even tripled, while defensive depth was quadrupled. Within these areas, the number of infantry troops doubled per frontline kilometre, while there was a six- to ten-fold increase in mortars and artillery, and an eight- to ten-fold rise in the number of tanks and self-propelled guns. Of more significance to Il-2 crews was the fact that the Germans at least doubled the number of anti-aircraft guns in the field.

This German troop train was attacked by Il-2s whilst stopped at Maloyaroslavets station on the Western Front in early 1942

In response, the Soviets raised the number of Il-2s per frontline kilometre six- to seven-fold when compared with numbers during the war's opening phases. Now there were up to 80 aircraft per frontline kilometre! Such numbers were required if German defences were to be suppressed. Il-2s delivered massive air strikes in regimental and divisional strength, these attacks being conducted as a sequence of strikes or as a single massive assault.

For a sequence of attacks, two to four groups each comprising 20 to 30 Il-2s reached the target in a column of four or six aircraft. Once there, the entire leading group carried out diving attacks. On recovery, they circled around to prepare for another attack. The other groups followed suit. These strikes could last for up to 90 minutes.

In a simultaneous all-out strike, targets were attacked by groups of six to eight Il-2s flying in a 'column of groups' combat formation totalling anywhere between 60 to 100 aircraft. Groups attacked simultaneously, which in turn meant that individual aircraft only spent a short time over the target, preventing crews from expending all their ammunition. Such attacks also caused considerable difficulties when it came to reassembling the column. On the credit side, such attacks had a shattering impact on enemy morale, and greatly reduced losses to fighters and flak.

Depending on the nature of the target, each group of Il-2s would form up in echelon and aircraft would then attack individually. The combat formation usually adopted by Il-2 groups was based on a pair, formed up in line abreast, in echelon formation or as a 'column of groups'.

CROWDED AIRSPACE

The deployment of Il-2s in such large groups in the final year of the war meant that commanders had to solve the problem of crowded airspace over the battlefield. Combat tactics therefore shifted from the regular circle formation to one that was more strung-out, extending up to eight kilometres (five miles) over the frontline and five kilometres (three miles) in depth. Up to 17 groups, each comprising four Il-2s, made four runs on the target within an hour, and without interfering with each other. This meant that *Shturmoviks* could conduct up to 270 attacks on targets on the battlefield over several hours, maintaining a constant presence over the enemy.

After a preliminary bombardment, Il-2s often laid smoke screens within which friendly forces could advance. But this was a complex and

A *Shturmovik* is armed with a 100-kg FAB-100 high-explosive bomb prior to flying a combat sortie. This particular weapon was a favourite amongst Il-2 regiments, which usually armed their aircraft with four FAB-100s per mission

dangerous task, as the screen had to be laid on time and at a precise location in order for it to be effective, and the aircraft had to fly at extremely low level without deviating from a straight course. Any break in the screen could expose attacking infantry to heavy losses. Due to their importance, and dangerous nature, such missions were only assigned to volunteers with plenty of experience.

During a breakthrough by attacking infantry, Il-2s were assigned the task of providing close air support to armour and motorised rifle units throughout the operation. The aircraft were ordered to stay over the battlefield to attack defending troops, artillery and armour ahead of, and flanking, the advancing forces. When the first two enemy trenches had been secured, the attack aircraft faced their toughest task. They then had to target any previously undetected emplacements, batteries or tanks to suppress them, thus preventing counter-attacks. The air strikes had to be delivered with pinpoint accuracy. At the same time, the diameter of the circle of Il-2s involved in these strikes could not exceed one to two kilometres (0.6-1.3 miles) so that the crews kept the target in sight and delivered a non-stop attack.

As Soviet forces slashed through enemy defences and encircled German formations, VVS KA's top priority was to provide close air support by delivering separate and concentrated air strikes against enemy positions. These tactics succeeded in raising the efficiency of such missions flown by the Il-2s in comparison with those performed in 1941-42 by a factor of six or even eight. This produced a similar improvement in the rate of advance by Soviet ground troops, and duly prevented German forces countering these attacks by either regrouping their forces or deploying reserves.

A key factor in the high level of effectiveness in the close air support role achieved by Il-2 units was that VVS KA had established strategic air superiority over the battlefield, giving the *Shturmovik* units considerable freedom of action. One result was a significant cut in the Il-2 loss rate. In 1943, one aircraft was lost for every 26 combat sorties flown, but by 1944-45 that rate had fallen to one loss for every 85-90 sorties completed.

The entire wartime experience shows that the Il-2 was highly effective in providing support for Soviet infantry, and that it represented one of the most formidable adversaries faced by the Germans. The aircraft's significance constantly increased as its role expanded, and there was a corresponding rise in VVS KA Il-2 strength.

Upon the outbreak of war in June 1941, Il-2s accounted for less than 0.2 per cent of the overall number of Soviet tactical combat aircraft. By autumn 1942 this figure had risen to 31 per cent, and it was maintained at 29 to 32 per cent through to May 1945. By contrast, the proportion of day bombers in the Red Air Force never exceeded 14 or 15 per cent. In other words, the Il-2 formed the main attack force of VVS KA.

The marks carefully applied on the armoured windscreen (a) and armoured engine cowling (b) of this Il-2 were to assist the pilot in his low-level bomb aiming. The aircraft's VV-1 sight can also be seen behind the windscreen

A clearer view of the VV-1 sight fitted to the Il-2, showing (1) the crosshairs and (2) the foresight

BIRTH OF
A LEGEND

The legend of the Guards attack units was born on 27 June 1941 when, five days after German forces invaded the Soviet Union, Il-2 armoured attack aircraft went into action for the first time. This historic action took place at 1940 hrs on the Sloutskiy Highway near Bobruysk, close to the River Berezina, when five Il-2s from 4th ShAP (formerly 4th BBAP) attacked a convoy of tanks and mechanised infantry from General Heinz Guderian's 2nd Panzer Group. Approaching the enemy force at low level, the *Shturmovik* pilots dropped their bombs and launched their rocket projectiles without bothering to use their sights – at that height, such a large convoy was hard to miss.

Capt Kholobaev's Il-2 encountered a battery of anti-aircraft guns and was seriously damaged, its armoured hull being torn open and the oil tank damaged. A huge shell-hole was also punched through the wing centre section that was so big that as Kholobaev eased himself out of the cockpit after landing, he fell through it. Hero of the Soviet Union (HSU) V B Emelyanenko recalls that when the regimental CO, Maj S G Getman, saw the state of Kholobaev's Il-2, he ordered it to be pushed into a hangar to hide it from view. However, prior to the order being carried out a Tupolev SB bomber crashed into the *Shturmovik* while making an emergency landing. Kholobaev's Il-2 was the regiment's first loss. Other aircraft sustained damage during the attack, but they were repaired.

4th ShAP's Il-2s were in action again during the small hours of the following day when they attacked German mechanised infantry and tank convoys and destroyed bridges across the Berezina, near Bobruysk. By the end of the day, the regiment had destroyed or damaged up to 20 armoured vehicles and halted the enemy's advance for six hours.

On 29 and 30 June, 4th ShAP continued to strike the *Wehrmacht* in the area, with attacks being delivered by small groups of Il-2s in relays. The last day of the month saw the regiment target weapons emplacements on the western bank of the river. Following a series of successful attacks, a Soviet detachment led by Gen Povetkin crossed the Berezina River and liberated Bobruysk. As a result of the regiment's success, Marshals Shaposhnikov and Voroshilov reported to Stalin, 'Our soldiers and commanding officers highly appreciate the Il-2. We ask to be provided with more such aircraft'. On 2 July the regiment received a commendation from the Western Front Commander, Marshal Timoshenko, for having destroyed nine crossings over the Berezina that same day.

But 4th ShAP had paid dearly for its success, having lost 19 pilots (13 were killed in the attack on the bridges alone) and 21 Il-2s. Deputy squadron leader Snr Lt V Ya Shirokiy had perished during a raid on the river crossings on 2 July, his aircraft being hit by flak and the pilot then

diving the burning Il-2 into a convoy of tanks and lorries. He was not
alone, for 11 other pilots failed to
return too. The men killed were
Snr Lts Sigida and Golubev (both
deputy squadron leaders), Bulavin,
Gotgelf and Sleptsov (flight leaders), Lts Pushin and Valkovich and
Jnr Lts Gritsevich, Podlobniy, Lap-
shov and Volkov.

Despite these losses, at dawn on
3 July, 4th ShAP bombed an enemy
airfield in Bobruysk. According to
the pilots involved, the sight that
greeted them resembled an airshow,

**Commander of 4th ShAP (from
7 March 1942, 7th GShAP), Hero of
the Soviet Union Maj S G Getman,
briefs regimental pilots before
another combat sortie on the
Southern Front in October 1941**

with aircraft parked in two rows on both sides of the runway, wing-tip to
wing-tip, and without any protective camouflage. The regiment delivered
its attack at full strength, although by that time it had only 19 serviceable
Il-2s, which was less than a third of its designated strength. Two groups
strafed aircraft in a single run across the airfield, and as they withdrew, the
Soviet pilots saw black smoke billowing from the target area. They in turn
could now assess the damage they had suffered during the attack.

The aircraft from the leading flight of the first group, comprising Maj
Getman, Senior Political Officer Vasilenko and deputy squadron leader
Sen Lt Koshelev, had been riddled with small arms fire. Indeed, those Il-2s
flown by Vasilenko and Koshelev crashed into a forest near the target,
while Getman limped home, despite his *Shturmovik* being damaged. It
was later learned that Vasilenko had survived the crash as a PoW, and
although later liberated by Red Army soldiers, such was the treatment he
received during his captivity that he became ill and never flew again.

The second group was also badly mauled, losing Senior Political
Officer Dryukov and Jnr Lts Krivich and Alekseykin.

4th ShAP attacked the airfield at Bobruysk three more times, and
reconnaissance photos of the site revealed that the regiment had damaged
20 to 23 bombers and 30 to 35 Bf 109s. It is likely, however, that these
tallies were exaggerated in official documents. The results of bombing
range tests, combined with analysis of Il-2 combat operations, suggested
that 30 aircraft at most would have been destroyed in four bomb strikes.

The considerable losses in both personnel and aircraft experienced by
4th ShAP in these early missions had been due to several factors. The
enemy's total air superiority and the Il-2's lack of defence against attacks
from behind had played their part, as had the poor organisation displayed
by the escorting fighters, the lack of tactical and flight training for
Shturmovik pilots and poor teamwork at flight level. The end result of
all of this was the loss of 40 aircraft by 4th ShAP in just 12 days of combat
operations. Nine more aircraft had sustained heavy damage and had to be
sent to field workshops for repairs to be effected.

As a result of this carnage, the regiment could field only ten serviceable
Il-2s and 18 pilots by the start of the Battle of Smolensk, which opened on
the morning of 10 July. After a total of 427 combat sorties, the regiment
handed its three remaining Il-2s to 215th ShAP, which had arrived in the

frontline at Pisarevka airfield on 20 August. 4th ShAP was then withdrawn to Voronezh, where it reformed.

Soviet forces remained very much on the back foot well into mid-August 1941, as the Red Army had been unable to establish a stable strategic defensive front. Equipped with 30 Il-2s, 215th ShAP had arrived just time in time to counter the 7th Panzer Division's powerful attack on the 19th Army near Dukhovshchina on 21 August. Every available aircraft in the area was thrown into blunting the attack.

Having only landed at Pisarevka 24 hours earlier, 215th ShAP had little time to prepare itself for action. In an effort to help the regiment overcome its combat inexperience, Western Front Air Force commander Col Naumenko ordered that one of the regiment's squadrons of ten Il-2s be temporarily attached to 61st ShAP, which had been fighting since 10 July. At the same time, some of 61st ShAP's more experienced pilots, led by the squadron leader Capt Filatov, were seconded without their aircraft to 215th ShAP in order 'to share their combat experience'.

During the early Il-2 missions against the 7th Panzer Division, the attack aircraft were led into action by Pe-2s from 140th SBAP and escorted by LaGG-3s and MiG-3s from 129th IAP. A total of three regimental-strength attacks were flown in a day, with strikes being delivered in sequence, one flight after another. These large-scale attacks were typically separated by intervals of up to one hour.

215th ShAP's combat score was opened by the regiment's deputy CO, Capt Gvozdev, when he flew a solo reconnaissance mission in the Plyushchevo-Losevo area on the morning of 21 August. Spotting a motorised convoy, Gvozdev turned back, but flak damaged his aircraft's control surfaces and it took all his skill to return to base and land safely. After making his report, Gvozdev led nine Il-2s to attack the convoy.

By this time, the vehicles were 20 km (13 miles) northeast of Dukhovshchina, and the Soviet attack aircraft attacked immediately with bombs, rockets and gunfire. Gvozdev's group was followed by another eight Il-2s, headed by the regimental CO, Maj L D Reyno, and preceded by a Pe-2 bomber and escorted by fighters. That evening, 215th ShAP received a message from Western Front Commander, Marshal Timoshenko, who praised the regiment, and particularly Gvozdev, for the successes they had achieved. Gvozdev was in action again the following day when he led seven Il-2s to inflict heavy losses on German forces in the Zamyatino-Kalugino-Shchelkino area. Another group of eight Il-2s, led by Capt Mamoshin, which had taken off a little later, managed to destroy ten enemy tanks and set several fuel tankers ablaze in the same area.

In two days the Il-2s of 61st ShAP and 215th ShAP had flown 82 combat sorties, compared with 69 by the MiG-3s and LaGG-3s of 129th IAP and the Pe-2s of 140th SBAP. The end result of all these missions was

Pictured here on the Western Front in August 1941 are pilots of 215th ShAP (6th GShAP from 6 December 1941). They are, from left to right, Capts S I Mironenko and I Glukhovtsev, Lt L Zatsepa, 47th SAD CO Col M V Kotelnikov, Snr Sgt V Zhukov, Jnr Lt A Dikin and unknown

the repulsing of the German attack. With the Il-2 pilots, and their fighter escorts, being singled out for particular praise by the Western Front Air Force CO, Col Naumenko, who sent the following congratulatory message to Col Tolstikov, CO of 47th SAD;

'I am extremely pleased with the successful operations conducted by attack aircraft and fighters. The counterattack by the enemy panzer division was repulsed due to your crushing blows on 21 and 22 August 1941. I am sure that further successful missions will result in the complete destruction of the Nazi panzer division. I hereby award a citation to the entire personnel of the division.'

On the 23rd Marshal Timoshenko attributed this success to the joint efforts made by both the ground and air forces;

'The glorious 64th and 50th Rifle Divisions spearheading our front, and the gallant 47th Air Division (61st ShAP, 215th ShAP and 129th IAP) destroying Nazi tanks, forced the enemy to withdraw in disorder. The enemy lost up to 130 tanks, in excess of 100 vehicles, a great number of guns and munitions and thousands of troops.'

Indirect confirmation of German losses suffered by the 7th Panzer Division came from the chief of the *Oberkommando des Heeres, OKH* (Army General Staff), who issued the following report on the condition of Army Group Centre on 28 August;

'The number of trucks in the inventory of the motorised divisions has been halved, and reduced by a quarter in reserve units and infantry divisions. 2nd Panzer Group units are left with an average of 45 per cent of their tank strength. 7th Panzer Division, 3rd Panzer Group, has only 24 per cent of its organic strength, while other divisions have 45 per cent. Divisions of 4th Panzer Group are better placed, having an average of 50 to 75 per cent of their tanks left.'

At the same time, 7th Panzer Division's strength was less than half that of the 3rd Panzer Group's 20th, 12th and 19th Panzer Divisions.

STRIKE NEAR LAKE ZHIZHITSA

The most notable combat sortie flown by aircraft from 215th ShAP during this period is listed in Red Army historical texts simply as the 'air strike near Lake Zhizhitsa'. Official 215th ShAP documentation gives a brief description of that day's events in typically dry military prose;

'On 30 August 1941, Maj Reyno led a group of six Il-2s, escorted by six fighters, to destroy an enemy convoy on the Lovanino-Eliseevo-

Il-2s could operate from unprepared airfields, which meant that country roads or forest clearings were often used as deployment sites for attack aircraft. This photograph was taken just west of Moscow in the autumn of 1941

Kostino-Selintsy road. On their way to the target, the Soviet group detected a concentration of enemy mechanised forces at newly-constructed river crossings over the Zhizhitsa River near Spitsyno, Kochegarovo and Lake Zhizhitsa. Maj Reyno took the initiative and decided to deal a crushing blow to the enemy troops. The attack resulted in the destruction of 15 tanks, 70 lorries and six guns, as well as the deaths of up to 580 troops.

'After avoiding heavy flak, Maj Reyno gathered his group and destroyed two bridges in his second run over the target area. The decisive action of Maj Reyno allowed the Soviet side to detect a new group of enemy forces and an axis of advance previously unknown to the front command, as well as to destroy enemy crossing points across the Zhizhitsa River and contain the enemy advance. Maj Reyno and his flight crews demonstrated exceptional courage, initiative, and resourcefulness.'

Two more Il-2 groups, headed by Capts Pakhnin and Gvozdev, attacked enemy troops near Lake Zhizhitsa that same day. Gvozdev and Lt Voloshin shared in the destruction of a Ju 87 during the course of their mission. Again, the scale of the enemy losses mentioned in the official Soviet document are not supported by the results of Il-2 armament range tests available to the Author, nor by combat efficiency evaluations made by special commissions between 1943 and 1945, when the Red Army was on the offensive, and could send inspectors and experts to the battlefield.

The archives of the units participating in combat operations during August 1941 reveal an interesting feature of damage assessments used for evaluating the efficiency of Soviet attack units. Regimental reports listed the number of large explosions and fires, or, occasionally, of directs hits on tanks and other vehicles reported by flight crews. Given the speed involved in such attacks and the hostile nature of the target environments, pilots could not provide more precise information. Yet divisional reports stated that hundreds of enemy troops had been killed and that dozens of tanks, vehicles and artillery pieces had been destroyed. While not trying to denigrate the heroism of Soviet pilots, it is probable that enemy losses were exaggerated by at least a factor of two and possibly by as much as five.

Not every sortie turned out to be a success, exaggerated or otherwise. On 31 August, group leader Capt Tarasov had difficulty in finding his designated target, as he had been given approximate coordinates only. When a group of five Il-2s approached the expected location of a German tank convoy, it was nowhere to be seen. As the leader searched for the target, banking sharply to starboard and port, the Il-2s suddenly found themselves above a heavily-defended convoy.

Suffering initial losses to flak, more Il-2s were downed when a hastily-flown attack proved ineffective due the aircraft having become dispersed, making them to easy prey for marauding German fighters.

An Il-2's engine is prepared for starting prior the aircraft flying a combat sortie in December 1941. The *Shturmovik* belonged to 57th PShAP of the Baltic Fleet Air Force. By order of the People's Commissar of the Navy, dated 1 March 1943, 57th PShAP became 7th GPShAP

23

The situation was only saved by the experience and self-control of the pilots involved, particularly their leader. The survivors closed ranks and reached friendly territory by flying at low level.

Capt Gvozdev, who was one of the regiment's most experienced Il-2 pilots, was killed leading a group of five aircraft to attack German tanks and artillery at Vorotyshchino on the morning of 5 September. The Soviet pilots claimed to have destroyed or damaged ten tanks and a similar number of field guns, but Gvozdev's aircraft was hit as he withdrew from the target area. Keeping his Il-2 on course for Soviet territory, he made an emergency landing once he had crossed the frontline. Once Gvozdev was reached by Red Army troops, it was discovered that he had been fatally wounded by a direct hit and succumbed to his injuries soon after crash-landing. He was buried with military honours.

Soviet aviation units operating in the Western Front sustained many other losses in similarly fierce battles, and were ultimately powerless to stop German advances. Guderian's forces had cut behind the South-Western Front by 10 September to threaten Kharkov's industrial area and the Donetsk Basin. This manoeuvre came nine days after the Western Front launched a doomed offensive near Smolensk on 1 September that ultimately failed to attain the objectives set for it by the Supreme High Command General Headquarters due to a lack of troops and equipment.

As a result, the Western and Bryansk Fronts went on the defensive on 11 September, allowing the Germans to reinforce their Army Group Centre and resume the advance on Moscow. In a desperate attempt to defend the capital, Western Front Air Force HQ developed a plan targeting the enemy's largest airfields.

Such strikes represented the most demanding combat missions flown by Il-2 units during the war, as most of the bigger airfields were located at the limits of the *Shturmovik's* range when it was carrying a standard combat load. This increased the burden placed on participating pilots, who were told to follow a designated course to the target and then conduct their attacks without deviating from their pre-briefed orders.

Airfields were also strongly defended, and in 1941 a typical Luftwaffe base was protected by two to four medium and six to eight light anti-aircraft artillery batteries. This meant a total of up to 16 88 mm anti-aircraft guns and as many as 104 20 mm and 37 mm cannon, to say nothing of up to ten heavy machine guns, three sound detectors and two searchlights.

An Il-2 attacks a German mechanised convoy with phosphorus pellets on the Bryansk Front in August 1941

This German cargo vessel was damaged by Il-2s from 57th PshAP of the Baltic Fleet Air Force in late 1941

Contemporary official documents state that these batteries would zero in on areas of airspace through which it was expected that Soviet attack aircraft would pass on their way to and from the target. Even with just the light AAA, there was a three- to five-layer density of fire. Cannon fire was set to converge at altitudes of 150-200 m (500-650 ft), 300-400 m (1000-1300 ft), 500-600 m (1700-2000 ft), 800-900 m (2600-3000 ft) and so on. Heavy machine guns covered low altitudes of up to 500-600 m (1700-2000 ft), while medium air defence artillery monitored an altitude of 1000-1500 m (3250-5000 ft) and higher. These weapons would only open up when the Il-2s entered their designated airspace, gunners having been trained to hold their fire to avoid detection until the right moment.

And if that was not enough, the airfields were usually protected by four to six fighters. Moreover, the German attack warning system was very efficient, which meant that aircraft from other bases would also be hastily scrambled when an airfield was targeted.

Experience quickly showed that airfield attacks would only succeed if they were meticulously prepared. This meant thorough reconnaissance of the target areas, and their defensive systems, maintaining the element of surprise, proper coordination between Il-2s and their escorting fighters and the suppression of air defence systems, both at the target and en route.

Accordingly, 215th ShAP did its best to develop an effective plan to strike a German airfield near Smolensk on 15 September. It was decided to mount the attack at dusk when enemy aircraft were returning from combat missions. With Soviet aircraft having to land back at their bases in pitch darkness, only the most experienced pilots were selected to participate in the operation. The attack force therefore included the regimental CO, Maj Reyno, together with pilots Kurapov, Korobkin, Markov and Voloshin. All were familiar with the airfield at Smolensk, and the approaches to it. This time there would be no leading Pe-2 bomber, and the two flights of escorting fighters were ordered to fly above and at a considerable distance from the Il-2s so as to avoid betraying their position. Total surprise was the key to achieving success in this mission.

After take-off, the Il-2s quickly assumed a combat formation, rendezvoused with six 129th IAP MiG-3s and headed for the target. The formation approached the airfield from the northeast at precisely 1823 hrs and took the enemy by surprise. The anti-aircraft guns opened fire too late, allowing Reyno to dive on the target without opposition, and his wingmen immediately followed. They launched their rockets at aircraft parked on the northern and northwestern edges of the airfield, strafing them at the same time. Finally, the Soviet pilots dropped fragmentation and incendiary bombs as they pulled out of their dives. Reyno's aircraft was hit by flak, but the pilot managed to coax his damaged Il-2 over the frontline and make an emergency landing in Soviet-held territory.

Pilots from 215th ShAP returned to the same airfield to deliver another blow at 1230 hrs the following day. This time there were nine Il-2s, led by squadron leader Snr Lt Novikov and escorted by six LaGG-3s and 12 MiG-3s. This attack did not enjoy the element of surprise, however. The mission followed a standard pattern – attack aircraft led to the airfield by a Pe-2, which designated the target with its bombs. The aircraft encountered heavy flak on their approach to the airfield, but they attacked all the same.

According to debriefing reports, the strike resulted in the destruction of up to 20 aircraft on the ground, and a series of hangars housing others was set ablaze. German gunners managed to hit four Il-2s, and although Jnr Lts Grachev and Karabulin returned home with wounds, two pilots were reported missing. Karabulin had distinguished himself by making a solo attack after he had lagged behind the group on the approach to the airfield, his Il-2 bombing and strafing the base as the other *Shturmoviks* withdrew. Despite being on his own, and thus being an attractive target for flak gunners, Karabulin destroyed four Ju 87s and set a hangar alight. He was to become one of the regiment's first pilots to be awarded the coveted title of HSU.

According to the escorting fighter pilots, the two strikes on the Smolensk airfield had destroyed as many as 35 enemy bombers, as well as four fuel trucks, an ammunition dump, a hangar and four vehicles.

The second 215th ShAP pilot to become a HSU was Jnr Lt Korobkin following his 'display of outstanding valour' on 23 September. A veteran of 30 combat sorties, he was considered to be one of the more experienced pilots in the regiment. During an attack on German artillery units near Yartsevo, Korobkin's Il-2 was hit by a flak shell which penetrated the canopy and exploded inside the cockpit. Fragments crippled Korobkin's left arm, punctured his throat and ripped his forehead open.

Despite being virtually blinded by the blood pouring from his head wounds, and with the use of only one arm, Korobkin refused to give up. Gripping the control column between his legs, he led the group into the attack, ordering his pilots to turn back only after they had dropped their bombs on the target. Weak from the loss of blood, Korobkin managed to return to base, where he made a belly landing. Fellow pilots and groundcrew ran to the Il-2 and lifted the now unconscious Korobkin out of the cockpit. Although it took Korobkin a very long time to recover from his wounds, he was later awarded the title of the HSU for his deeds.

OPERATION *TYPHOON*

The Germans launched Operation *Typhoon* on 30 September with an attack on the left wing of the Bryansk Front, near Zhukovka-Shostka, by Guderian's 2nd Panzer Group and Weichs' 2nd Field Army. The main

Il-2 pilot Lt V F Zudilov was awarded the title of HSU on 2 August 1944. A veteran of several hundred *Shturmovik* combat sorties, he is seen here while serving with 6th GShAP in the autumn of 1941

forces of Army Group Centre included the 4th and 9th Field Armies and the 3rd and 4th Panzer Groups, headed by Generalfeldmarschall Fedor von Bock. On 2 October this force dealt a series of blows to the Western and Reserve Fronts from their staging areas north of Dukhovshchina and east of Roslavl. Initially, *Typhoon* was conducted with impeccable efficiency, enabling battle-worn divisions to re-group and restore combat effectiveness without Soviet reconnaissance aircraft detecting anything.

The Germans concentrated such powerful spearheads along the main axes of advance that Red Army units could not contain them. Indeed, the enemy hurled no fewer than 12 divisions and almost every available aircraft at the junction between the Western Front's 30th and 19th Armies, which was defended by Gen Dreer's 45th Cavalry Division. The result was that the Germans were able to focus an overwhelming superiority in manpower and equipment in the area chosen for the breakthrough.

The *Wehrmacht* deployed an average of two field divisions, supported by up to 60 tanks and 30 aircraft, for every four kilometres (2.5 miles) of the frontline. Ranged against them were two rifle battalions, six tanks, six anti-tank guns and 18 76 mm guns of the Red Army. Repulsing the German attack with such a force was a virtually impossible task. This is how no less an authority than Marshal Georgy Zhukov, the Soviet Deputy Supreme Commander, described this phase of the conflict;

'The Germans' striking power was a total surprise to us. A six- to eight-fold numerical superiority in the main axes of advance was also a surprise, which predetermined our losses in the first period of the war.'

The 4th Panzer Group captured Yukhnovo on the night of 5 October, and two days later it was on the outskirts of Vyazma, where it joined up with the 3rd Panzer Group's 7th Panzer Division. With this rendezvous completed, enemy forces now encircled the Soviet 19th, 20th, 24th and 32nd Armies, which comprised Gen Belov's group, and part of the 30th, 43rd and 49th Armies of the Western and Reserve Fronts.

With the Red Army desperately short of troops to seal widening gaps that were now appearing in its defensive lines to the west of Moscow, air power appeared to be the only way to contain a rampant enemy. Blunting the German advances was not going to be an easy task for the air regiments thrown into action, for an increase in the number of light artillery batteries in the frontline had significantly improved the effectiveness of the *Wehrmacht* army groups' and mechanised convoys' air defences.

According to captured documents seized by Soviet forces during this period, every German mechanised division had attached to it a battalion of 20 light flak comprising 27 37 mm and 18 20 mm cannon, plus up to 20 more batteries of 37 mm cannon in each mechanised regiment. They also deployed between 60-70 light machine guns at the head and rear of every convoy to engage low-flying Il-2s.

A German tank burns on the outskirts of Moscow after receiving a direct hit from a FAB-50 bomb dropped by an Il-2 during the dogged defence of the Soviet capital in December 1941

Given their lack of experience in attacking such well-defended targets, Il-2 units suffered grievous losses on almost every combat sortie. Those regiments attempting to halt the German advance on Moscow in October 1941 lost an average of one aircraft for every 8.6 combat sorties flown. Even so, pilots still managed to inflict significant losses on the enemy despite the environment in which they were operating.

For instance, a flight of Il-2s from 215th ShAP, escorted by six MiG-3s from 129th IAP, attacked a mechanised convoy near the village of Karpovo on 3 October. The aircraft dropped 12 FAB-50 bombs, expended 24 RS-132 rocket projectiles and fired 1000 ShVAK cannon rounds to destroy or damage up to 12 vehicles and two or three field artillery batteries. According to the unit's combat log, the group leader, Snr Lt A E Novikov, met a hero's death when he was shot down by flak over the target. Despite his aircraft being literally consumed by flames around him, Novikov crashed the blazing Il-2 into the German convoy.

A week later, 215th ShAP, which had lost a large number of its aircraft, was withdrawn from the frontline and sent to Kuybyshev to be reformed.

Sacrifices such as that made by Snr Lt Novikov ultimately proved not to be in vain, however, as by early December 1941 the German advance on Moscow had petered out due to troop exhaustion and a paucity of supplies. *Typhoon* failed to reach its objective. Army Group Centre was forced to go on the defensive along the frontline when the Kalinin, Western and the South-Western Fronts mounted a decisive counter-offensive on 5-6 December. Fearing encirclement, German units beat a hasty retreat, leaving much equipment, including heavy guns, behind.

On 6 December the People's Commissar of Defence ordered 215th ShAP to be transformed into 6th GShAP for the valour it had displayed in combat. The regiment therefore became the first Guards unit in VVS RKKA attack aviation. Many pilots were decorated with orders and medals, and regimental CO Maj L D Reyno became a HSU. The first to fly the Il-2 in action, 4th ShAP was also awarded the Guards title on 7 March 1942 when the regiment became 7th GShAP.

Just prior to 4th ShAP being withdrawn in August 1941 for reformation, regimental HQ had prepared recommendations for decorations to pilots who had distinguished themselves in combat. These documents were, however, burned in a bombing raid. On 17 September, 4th ShAP, equipped with 24 Il-2s and new pilots, flew from Voronezh to the Southern Front. Meanwhile, Gen Kravchenko, CO of 11th Combined Air Division, which had included 4th ShAP, had not forgotten those pilots recommended for decorations. Under a decree of the Presidium of the USSR Supreme Council, 4th ShAP received the Order of Lenin for the way it had discharged its duty, regimental CO Maj S G Getman became a HSU and 32 pilots and groundcrew were also decorated.

Pilots of 174th ShAP (15th GShAP from 7 March 1942) are seen with their patrons – workers from the Kirovskiy Factory – on the Leningrad Front in November 1941. Snr Lt F A Smyshlyaev is in the foreground, pointing at the tail of the Il-2

STALINGRAD

Following months of action and heavy losses, Il-2 units enjoyed the break in combat operations brought on by severe winter weather from November 1941 through to the spring of 1942. The first large-scale *Shturmovik* operations of the new year came when the South-Western Front mounted its offensive on Kharkov on 12 May. In an extremely risky two-pronged operation, the Red Army intended to deal one blow against the enemy from Volchansk and another from the Barvenkovo salient.

The Il-2 of 7th GShAP squadron leader Capt Shemyakin returns (note the empty rocket rails) from a combat mission on the Southern Front in March 1942

However, just five days into the operation, 11 German divisions of Army Group Kleist breached the defensive positions of the Southern Front's 9th and 57th Armies in the Slavyansk-Kramatorsk area and drove swiftly into the South-Western Front's left flank. By 19 May German forces had reached the rear of the South-Western Front, and by the 23rd the Barvenkovo salient had been completely encircled.

In an attempt to avert disaster, VVS RKKA command and the Supreme High Command General Headquarters hastily reinforced the air forces in the danger zone. A total of seven fighter and two attack aircraft regiments (243rd and 766th ShAP) arrived in the South-Western Front. By 22 May, 94th BAP, 820th ShAP and 429th IAP had been attached to 220th IAD (*Istrebitelniy Aviatsionniy Polk* – Fighter Air Regiment), but as early as the 29th, these regiments, plus 505th ShAP, were reassigned to Col V V Stepichev's 228th ShAD.

That same day, 619th ShAP was included in the frontline air group, while the Su-2-equipped 826th BBAP had gone into action two days earlier. By late May, 4th Air Army of the Southern Front comprised 230th ShAD, 216th, 217th and 229th IAD, 218th NBAD (*Nochnoi Bombardirovshchiuk Aviatsionniy Polk* – Night Bomber Air Regiment), 219th BAD (*Bombardirovshchiuk Aviatsionniy Polk* – Bomber Air Regiment) and seven combined air regiments. Lt Col Getman had been appointed CO of the new 230th ShAD on the 18th.

7th GShAP CO, Maj K N Kholobaev, was photographed in the cockpit of his Il-2 on the Southern Front in March 1942

To strike a blow against the Luftwaffe it was decided to attack its primary airfields. In the vanguard of these missions on 25 May was a flight of Il-2s from 7th GShAP of 230th ShAD, comprising Snr Lt Mospanov, Lt Boyko and Jnr Lt Artemov. They were sent to attack aircraft on an airfield near Konstantinovka, which fresh reconnaissance photos had shown was home to up 90 aircraft of various types. The Il-2s approached from the southeast at extremely low level, before zoom-climbing up to 100-150 m (300-500 ft) and commencing their attack runs. Total surprise was achieved, the *Shturmoviks* having made three runs over the target area by the time the German flak gunners opened fire.

Future HSU V B Emelyanenko of 7th GShAP smiles for the camera at Khutor Smeliy airfield, on the Southern Front, in the Donetsk Basin in May 1942

Chief of staff of 7th GShAP, Maj F V Kozhukhovskiy (left foreground), and the regimental political officer, B E Ryabov (in the fur hat), brief pilots on the Southern Front in March 1942

Capt Ilya Mospanov of 7th GShAP distinguished himself in strikes on airfields in the Kharkov sector, being decorated for one particular attack he made on Konstantinovka airfield on 24 May 1942. According to Il-2 crews, the regiment's attack resulted in the destruction or damage of 26 aircraft. Mospanov is seen here at Khutor Smeliy airfield, on the Southern Front, in the Donetsk Basin in May 1942

Upon returning to base, the pilots involved claimed to have damaged 22 aircraft, setting some of them on fire. Mospanov was recommended for the Order of Lenin (his third decoration) for leading the mission.

At dawn on 27 May, six Il-2s from 431st ShAP, escorted by seven Yak-1s from 273rd IAP, attacked Chuguev airfield – some 50 aircraft were reported to be based there. Surprise was again achieved, with the Soviet pilots spotting flightcrews lined up in front of their aircraft for an inspection as they made their attack runs. The defending gunners did not open fire until the Soviet aircraft were on their way home, having dropped their bombs and strafed the airfield. Two patrolling Bf 109s tried to attack the Il-2s, but they were downed by escorting fighters. According to the Soviet pilots, 20 German aircraft had been destroyed or damaged.

Three days later, 504th ShAP and 800th ShAP from 226th ShAD, commanded by Col M I Gorlachenko, were in action. Six Il-2s from 800th ShAP, led by Capt Rusakov, delivered an effective attack on Kursk-Zapadniy airfield, home to 40 aircraft. Escorted by ten LaGG-3s from 31st IAP, they struck between 0715-0720 hrs. This time the flak was heavy, but the Il-2s and their escorts claimed to have destroyed or damaged 15 enemy aircraft. On their way home, the LaGG-3s engaged in a fierce dogfight with German fighters. Capt Krasnov was shot down but survived, while Lt Bystrov was reported missing in action. The following morning, crews from 800th ShAP attacked Kursk-Vostochniy airfield.

Over the next ten days, South-Western Front aircraft flew a further three strikes on six German airfields. Half of these attacks were made by Il-2s, including the raid on Stalino airfield by 12 *Shturmoviks* from 7th GShAP and 210th ShAP. Appearing over the base just as the German aircraft were preparing for a combat sortie, the Soviet attack pilots spotted around 50 He 111 and Ju 88 twin-engined bombers parked in large groups being refuelled from tankers. The Soviet aircraft came in at low-level with the sun behind them, and following their attack runs, the effectiveness of the Il-2s' bombing and strafing was confirmed by the crew of a reconnaissance aircraft that overflew the airfield immediately after the *Shturmoviks*. At least 20 German aircraft had been destroyed.

Two Bf 109s that were attempting to take-off when the Soviet aircraft arrived on the scene were also shot down by the group's leader, Maj N A Zub. These successes forced the Luftwaffe to send its 4th

Air Fleet to the rear to regroup, and resulted in a slackening of German aerial activity in the area.

In addition to striking airfields, the Il-2s also attacked tank and motorised convoys near Mospanov, Volchiy Yar, Mikhailovka and Grakovo, as well as bridges over rivers such as the Severskiy Donets, Tavolzhanka and Staritsa. These attacks, however, were to end in failure due to serious planning flaws which seriously undermined the combat efficiency of the units involved. Gen Falaleev, commander

of South-Western Front aviation, explained the major shortcomings in a report written in the wake of these missions;

'There is a tendency to operate in small groups. This is one of our major mistakes. A small group is easily contained by the enemy. It loses the initiative, disperses and suffers losses, since its aircraft fight independently. Bombers and attack aircraft do not manoeuvre when attacked by enemy fighters. They keep on flying in a straight line and become strung out, which affects their mutual fire support.

'Targets are usually attacked in a single run, with munitions dropped in a salvo. Regimental commanders, assigning close air support, bomb and attack missions, do not specify the exact number of runs to be made, or the time to turn back for home.

'Our attack aircraft and bombers do not always make enemy tanks their priority targets, preferring instead to attack lorries, carts and other less important targets. Flight briefing is poor. Mission objectives are not clear or specific. Regimental commanding officers usually specify the target area and appoint flight crews to discharge the task.

'Unit commanders do not bear proper responsibility for fulfilling combat missions. Causes of losses are not analysed or determined. Unit commanders do not bear any liability for losses caused by poor pre-flight preparation and briefing or ill-organised mutual fire support.'

On several occasions, badly-organised missions resulted in Red Army losses on the ground. For example, on 26 May aircraft from 230th ShAD attacked an area near Chepel where friendly tanks were engaged in a battle

Pilots of 7th GShAP pose in front of the aircraft flown by their squadron leader, Maj N A Zub (seen here closest to the camera), on the Southern Front in March 1942. The titling on the Il-2's fuselage reads *Smert Fashistskim Okkupantam* ('Death to Fascist Invaders')

with the enemy. The Soviet tanks were forced to halt their attack while the Il-2s targeted German forces, and when the *Shturmoviks* left, Luft-waffe bombers, operating in groups of 20 to 30, appeared over the battle-field. They immediately targeted the now stationary Soviet tank forma-tions, inflicting serious losses.

On 9 June the People's Commissar of Defence ordered the air forces of the South-Western Front to be

Il-2s fly over a German river crossing on the South-Western Front in July 1942. Strikes on these crossings were amongst the most demanding missions flown by attack aircraft pilots, as these structures were usually heavily protected by anti-aircraft artillery and Luftwaffe fighter patrols

During the summer of 1942 pilots and groundcrews of attack aircraft regiments converted single-seat Il-2s into two-seat aircraft and armed them with 12.7 mm UBT or 7.62 mm ShKAS machine guns for rear defence against German fighters. About 1200 single-seaters were modified in such a way. In this photograph, Il-2 air gunner Sgt Baklar Saakyan is strapped in behind a makeshift ShKAS defensive machine gun mounting, which appears to have come from a Tupolev SB-2 medium bomber

combined under the command of Gen Khryukin. The 8th Air Army comprised 268th, 269th, 220th, and 206th IAD, 228th and 226th ShAD, 270th and 271st BAD and 272nd NBAD. 235th IAD, six independent fighter regiments and four combined air regiments had been transferred to the 8th Air Army from the Supreme High Command reserves and other fronts by 13 June 1942. All these units were at half-strength, however, and the proportion of unserviceable aircraft reached 40 to 50 per cent, leaving Khryukin unable to contain German tank and motorised convoys. This meant that on 13 June, the 8th Air Army was only able to detail 20 Il-2s and 18 day bombers to provide close air support for ground troops.

Despite only being in action for just under a month, one of the units to suffer the most losses during this period was Lt Col Shishkin's 800th ShAP. With its surviving pilots exhausted and only a handful of Il-2s still operable, the unit was sent to be reformed in mid-June. It was replaced by battle-hardened 505th ShAP, commanded by Maj Chumachenko. 800th ShAP's remaining aircraft, together with a squadron of new machines ferried straight from the factory, were combined with aircraft drawn from Maj Boldyrikhin's 504th ShAP to bring 505th ShAP up to full strength.

At the same time, 228th ShAD was reinforced by the combat-ready 431st and 285th ShAPs from the 4th Reserve Air Group and the Front Manoeuvre Air Group, respectively. Both groups were then disbanded, while the remaining 243rd and 619th ShAPs were withdrawn to the rear. On 5 July, Khryukin ordered 226th and 228th ShADs to be redeployed to Bobrov rear area airfield to be reformed too. Both divisions returned to the front on the 15th. Forty-eight hours earlier, the 8th Air Army had also received 206th ShAD, which comprised 811th, 873rd and 621st ShAPs.

MORE ENEMY ADVANCES

Despite the efforts of the 8th Air Army command to reorganise and bolster the strength of the attack aviation regiments in its area, the efficiency of the close air support remained poor and German panzer groups continued their swift advance towards the strategically important Soviet city of Stalingrad. The enemy had reached the outward defensive positions in the Plodovitoe-Abganerovo area by 5 August.

Aerial engagements during this time were extremely fierce, and resulted in heavy attack aircraft losses. Despite the odds being stacked against the Il-2 units, their pilots fought on, displaying outstanding valour.

One such engagement took place on 24 July, when 688th ShAP pilot Sgt Shot was bounced by two Bf 109s after he had attacked his target. His aircraft sustained extensive damage to its starboard landing gear, starboard wing centre section, two propeller blades and control cables. Shot was also badly wounded in the right eye, yet he managed to reach

Maj N A Zub of 7th GShAP was credited with shooting down two Bf 109s during an attack on Stalino airfield in early June 1942. This photograph was taken several months later, and the strain of the spring and summer fighting is etched all over his face. At that time, 7th GShAP formed part of Reserve Air Group No 5 (RAG-5). Zub achieved fame for his pinpoint attacks on enemy troops and equipment during this period, and he was later made CO of 210th ShAP. A veteran of 381 combat sorties, Maj Zub was eventually killed over the Blue Line on 22 July 1943. He was posthumously awarded the title of HSU

a Soviet-held airfield and landed successfully, although he then lost consciousness.

On 4 August a group of five Il-2s from 504th ShAP, 226th ShAD, led by Snr Lt Pstygo and escorted by 11 Yak-1s from 148th IAP, took off to reconnoitre and attack panzers southwest of Stalingrad. The Yaks became embroiled in a dogfight with five Bf 109s over the reconnaissance area and lost sight of the attack aircraft they were supposed to be escorting. Pstygo's Il-2s nevertheless reached the Aksay-Abganerovo road, where they came across a large convoy of tanks, together with many troops.

Having photographed the convoy and then commenced their attacks, the *Shturmoviks* were bounced by 20 Bf 109s. Every Il-2 was effectively destroyed in the ensuing battle, although three made crash-landings. But this success was not without cost to the German pilots, as the *Shturmoviks* shot down two Bf 109s. The Messerschmitts crashed in Soviet-held territory, allowing Red Army units to confirm the Il-2 pilots' victories.

Three days later 622nd ShAP CO Maj Zemlyanskiy was killed in action while attacking German armour on the southern face of the Stalingrad outward defensive line. Coming under heavy anti-aircraft fire, which caused his Il-2 to burst into flames, Zemlyanskiy ordered his second-in-command to lead the group, then dived his burning aircraft into the enemy armour. By decree of the Presidium of the USSR Supreme Council, dated 5 November 1942, Zemlyanskiy was posthumously awarded the title of HSU.

Snr Sgt Rogalskiy, a young pilot from 673rd ShAP, repeated Zemlyanskiy's deed on 10 August when he was hit by flak near the Malaya Tinguta River. Rogalskiy's Il-2 caught fire and the pilot dived into a column of lorries, where it exploded. It was his first combat sortie.

8th Air Army Il-2s delivered attacks on airfields near Olkhovskoe, Podolkhovskoe and Oblivskoe on 12 August. The first blow was dealt by 13 Il-2s from 226th and 228th ShAD, escorted by two Yak-1s from 220th ShAD. Their target was Oblivskoe airfield, where 126 aircraft were reported to be based. At 0400 hrs Il-2s approached the airfield at low-level, zoomed upwards and then dived on the parked aircraft. German gunners opened fire after the *Shturmoviks* had made their first run over the target, but enemy fighters had no time to scramble. After expending all their ammunition, the Il-2s returned home without loss.

A little later, Il-2s from 686th ShAP, 206th ShAD, escorted by 12 Yak-1s from 269th IAD and five LaGG-3s from 235th IAD, attacked the airfields at Olkhovskoe and Podolkhovskoe. This time, however, the enemy was ready for them. Flying through a hail of defensive fire, the Il-2s attacked aircraft on the ground. During their second run they were attacked by 30 Bf 109s, which were in turn set upon by the *Shturmovik's* escort fighters. This distracted the German fighter pilots long enough for the Il-2s to attack the airfield.

While aircraft from 686th ShAP were withdrawing, the Bf 109s struck again, downing regimental CO Maj Zotov on their first pass – he returned to his unit with a burned face five days later. Jnr Lt Kiselkov shot down two Bf 109s by employing a scissors manoeuvre, but a machine gun burst at point-blank range in turn damaged his Il-2. Despite a head wound, Kiselkov was able to reach friendly territory and belly-land his aircraft near the village of Budenniy (*text continues on page 42*).

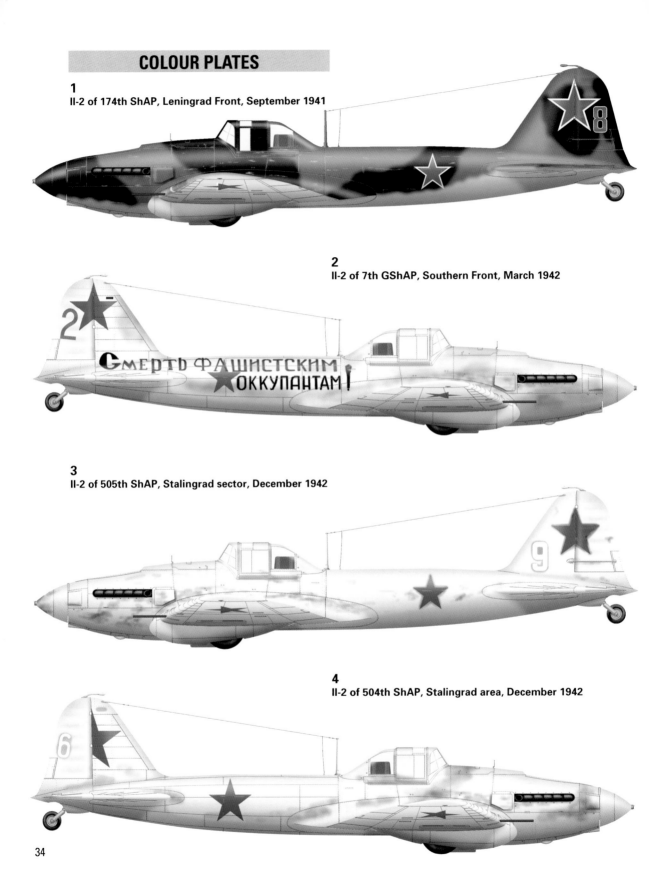

1
Il-2 of 174th ShAP, Leningrad Front, September 1941

2
Il-2 of 7th GShAP, Southern Front, March 1942

3
Il-2 of 505th ShAP, Stalingrad sector, December 1942

4
Il-2 of 504th ShAP, Stalingrad area, December 1942

5
Il-2 of 667th ShAP, Kalinin Front, January 1943

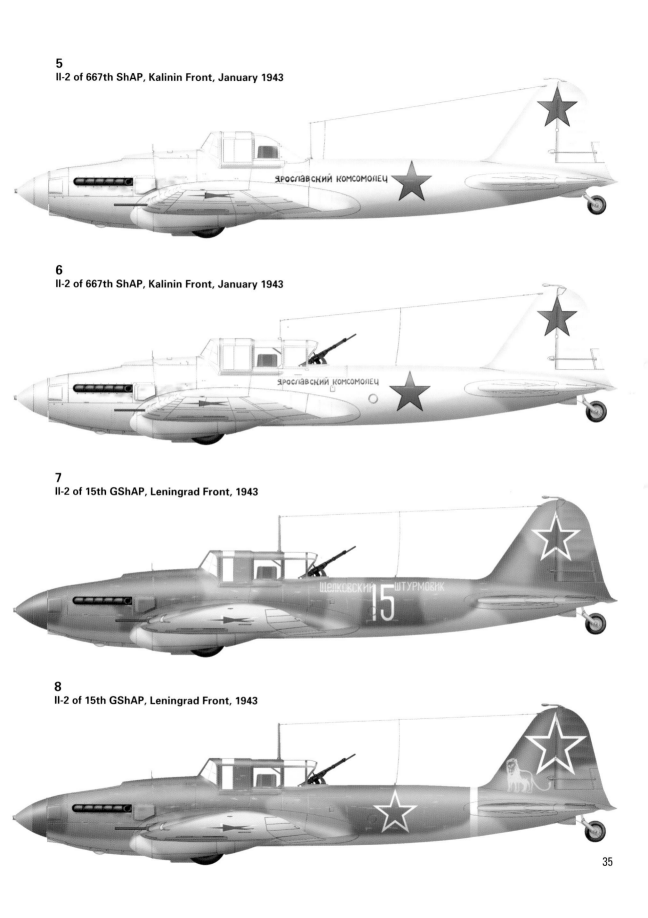

6
Il-2 of 667th ShAP, Kalinin Front, January 1943

7
Il-2 of 15th GShAP, Leningrad Front, 1943

8
Il-2 of 15th GShAP, Leningrad Front, 1943

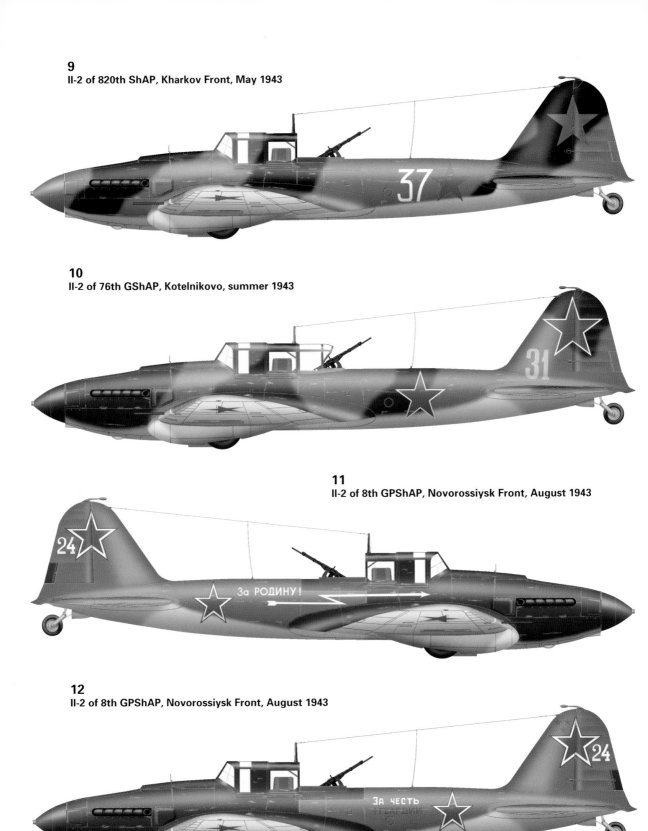

9
Il-2 of 820th ShAP, Kharkov Front, May 1943

10
Il-2 of 76th GShAP, Kotelnikovo, summer 1943

11
Il-2 of 8th GPShAP, Novorossiysk Front, August 1943

За РОДИНУ!

12
Il-2 of 8th GPShAP, Novorossiysk Front, August 1943

За ЧЕСТЬ ГВАРДИИ

13
Il-2 of 8th GPShAP, Saki, April 1944

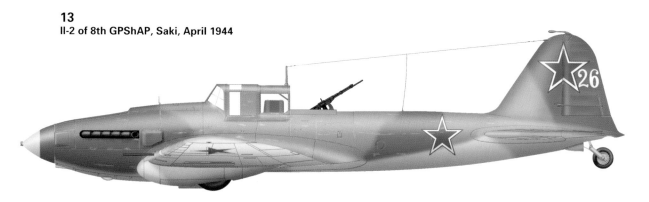

14
Il-2 of 7th GShAP, North Caucasus Front, summer 1943

15
Il-2 of 7th GShAP, North Caucasus Front, August 1943

16
Il-2 of 617th ShAP, Kharkov Front, August 1943

17
Il-2 of 15th GShAP, Leningrad Front, June 1944

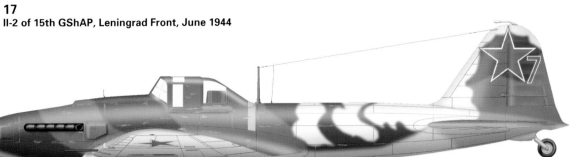

18
Il-2 of 90th GShAP, 1st Ukrainian Front, autumn 1944

19
Il-2 of 8th GPShAP, Crimea, April 1944

За женю ЛОБАНОВА

20
Il-2 of 108th GShAP, Crimea, May 1944

Полина Осипенко

21
Il-2-37 of 75th GShAP, Crimea, May-June 1944

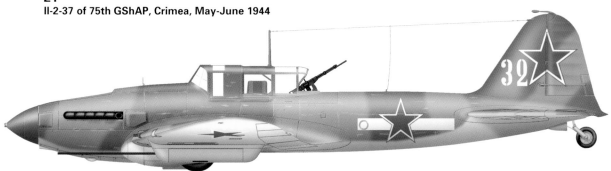

22
Il-2 of 75th GShAP, Crimea, May-June 1944

23
Il-2 of 140th GShAP, 2nd Ukrainian Front, summer 1944

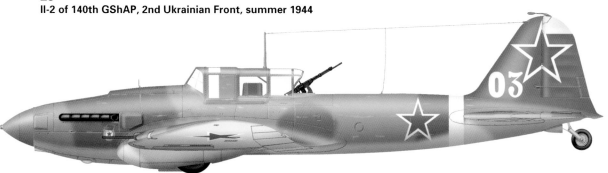

24
Il-2 of 6th GShAP, 1st Baltic Front, August 1944

25
Il-2 of 6th GShAP, 1st Baltic Front, August 1944

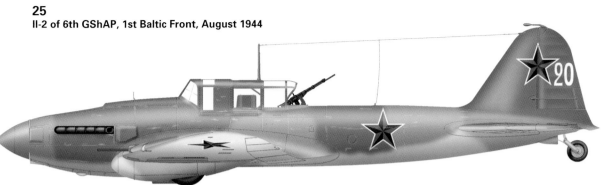

26
Il-2 of 154th GShAP, 3rd Byelorussian Front, autumn 1944

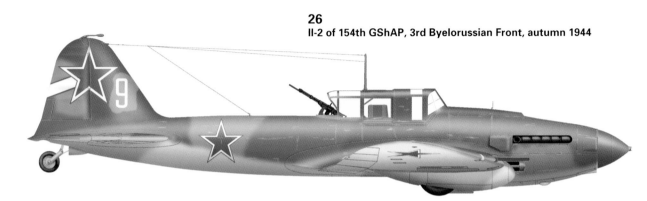

27
Il-2 of 154th GShAP, 3rd Byelorussian Front, autumn 1944

28
Il-2 of 154th GShAP, 3rd Byelorussian Front, autumn 1944

29
Il-2 of 6th GShAP, 1st Baltic Front, January 1945

30
Il-2 of 76th GShAP, 1st Baltic Front, January 1945

31
Il-2 of 76th GShAP, 1st Baltic Front, January 1945

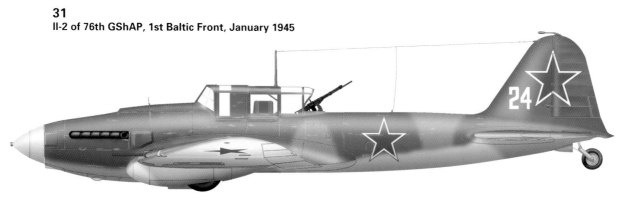

32
Il-2 of 90th GShAP, 1st Baltic Front, April 1945

Flight leader Lt Nebolsin also had to crash-land in Soviet-held territory near the village of Podstepnoe after his aircraft was hit five times and went out of control, while deputy squadron leader Snr Lt Toporkov was yet another to make an emergency landing. Squadron leader Capt Batrak and Sgts Mukhin and Smolyakov were killed in the dogfight with Luftwaffe fighters, the latter claiming seven Il-2s for the loss of three Bf 109s.

Despite 686th ShAP suffering badly at the hands of the *Jagdwaffe*, 8th Air Army headquarters claimed on the basis of reconnaissance data and flight crew debriefings that 89 German aircraft had been destroyed or damaged in the airfield attacks. Although doubt has been cast on this figure, a captured German airman was able to shed some light on the effect of the attacks. Unteroffizier R Holzer from the 16th Reconnaissance Group, 3rd Reconnaissance Detachment, who was captured on 14 August, had been near Oblivskoe during the Soviet attack two days before. Under interrogation, Holzer stated;

'The strike was so unexpected that none of the fighters were able to scramble, while the air defence gunners opened fire too late. The corps suffered heavy losses as a result. Our group alone lost 16 to 27 aircraft. I am not aware of the exact losses sustained by other groups, but they are slightly less significant than ours, since our area suffered the main blow. Immediately after the attack, we were ordered to prepare to take-off. The leaders of all groups were summoned by the command and, some time later, all but 11 aircraft left.

'The morale of flight personnel in my unit, which had been high at the time of our arrival at the front, was considerably undermined by the strikes. First and foremost, most of the flight crews were left without aircraft. Secondly, everyone realised that war in Russia was anything but a walkover, and that both ground and air units were suffering losses.'

The German Sixth Field Army and 4th Panzer Army mounted another offensive on Stalingrad on 17 August, resulting in fierce battles being fought on the outskirts of the city. On the morning of the 23rd, German troops, with massive Luftwaffe support, breached the Stalingrad Front between the 4th Tank Army and 62nd Army and started advancing on Rynok. By 1600 hrs, Gen von Wietersheim's XIV Panzer Corps had reached the Volga River in the Erzovka-Rynok area. This thrust drove an eight-kilometre (five-mile) wedge in the Soviet front. When they reached the Volga, the Germans turned south towards Stalingrad.

Due to a lack of aerial reconnaissance over the ever-changing frontline, the Soviets could not determine where and when the enemy had reached the river. It was not until 1730 hrs that Gen Khryukin ordered the commanders of 228th and 206th ShAD and 270th BAD to attack von Wietersheim's force. He issued the units with the following instructions;

'A large group of enemy tanks and motorised infantry is advancing from Erzovka to Stalingrad. Your orders are to immediately scramble your aircraft to destroy the enemy convoy and prevent it from reaching Stalingrad. Combat sorties are to be made until nightfall.'

As a result, the Il-2s immediately switched from attacking airfields to targeting German tanks and mechanised infantry near Erzovka, Rynok and Orlovka. Pilots demonstrated outstanding heroism and self-sacrifice as they flung themselves at the enemy in an effort to stall the German advance. During one such strike on tanks and infantry near Rynok, the

Il-2s pull away from their target over the Soviet steppe following a strafing run in the summer of 1942. It was at this point in their mission that the *Shturmoviks* were at their most vulnerable when it came to being attacked by *Jagdwaffe* fighters

deputy squadron leader of 766th ShAP, 206th ShAD, Jnr Lt Shevchenko, rammed his damaged Il-2 into a concentration of German forces.

But once again poor communication between some of the air divisions and 8th Air Army headquarters was to have tragic consequences. Between 1920 hrs and 1954 hrs on 23 August, seven Il-2s from 206th ShAD struck units of Gen Khasin's 23rd Tank Corps in the Erzovka area by mistake, inflicting severe losses. Things could have been far worse, however, as Gen Khryukin had not received a message sent by 272nd NBAD CO, Col Kuznetsov, stating that the Il-2s had in fact attacked friendly forces. As a result, 206th ShAD CO, Col Sryvkin, was ordered to make another attack on Erzovka. Fortunately, the sortie was cancelled just in time.

SOVIET FORCES RETREAT

Despite the best efforts of the Il-2 units, German forces breached 64th Army's defensive lines on 29 August and advanced north to threaten the rear of 62nd and 64th Armies. This forced the Stalingrad and South-Eastern Fronts to retreat first to the middle defensive line and then further east still to the inner defensive line. With the situation rapidly deteriorating, VVS RKKA command resorted to extreme measures.

On 4 September, the undermanned and under-equipped 16th Air Army, with its 79 Il-2s, 42 fighters and 31 bombers, was hurled into action. Ranged against it were the 1200 combat aircraft of the German 4th Air Fleet. The air battles were fierce, with almost every Il-2 combat sortie resulting in a dogfight with Luftwaffe fighters. There were heavy losses of both personnel and aircraft as a result.

At that time, attack aircraft regiments usually struck battlefield targets in squadron-strength of six to eight Il-2s, flying in echelon formation and making up to three bombing and strafing passes on their targets. Typically, the echelon would usually become a broken column of single aircraft – then called 'a string' – after the first run. As a result, Il-2 passes over the target became spaced out, and this denied the attacking aircraft mutual fire support. It also gave anti-aircraft gunners the opportunity to pour concentrated fire into the Il-2s as they made follow-up runs.

German fighters also had plenty of time to scramble and attack the Il-2s from their blind sectors below and behind. Stragglers and pilots who had lost their bearings were particularly easy meat for the fighters. Heavy losses were suffered by all attack regiments over Stalingrad as a result.

Moreover, it was virtually impossible for the Il-2s to deliver their strikes from medium altitude without fighter escort. But the attack aircraft had a hard time even when they were escorted because there was no two-way radio communication with the accompanying fighters. Loss statistics showed that Luftwaffe fighters accounted for 62 per cent of the Il-2s downed in the Stalingrad area. In an effort to avoid becoming a statistic, the most resolute Il-2 pilots soon realised that they had to engage in dogfights with enemy fighters.

And they did. Snr Sgt Danilov of 807th ShAP shot down a Bf 109 on 24 August, a Ju 88 the following day and a Bf 110 on 29 August. On the 30th, deputy squadron leader Snr Lt Kochetkov, one of the 686th ShAP's most seasoned pilots, shot down a Messerschmitt in a dogfight with Ju 87s and escorting Bf 110s. Kochetkov was killed three days later when his Il-2 took a direct hit from a heavy artillery round and exploded in

43

mid-air. By decree of the Presidium of the USSR Supreme Council, dated 5 November 1942, Kochetkov was posthumously made a HSU.

By 15 September German forces had penetrated Soviet defences at the junction of the 62nd and 64th Armies, captured the suburb of Kuporosnoe and reached the Volga. The city was now ringed by fighting. Three days later, pilots from 688th ShAP, 228th ShAD laid a smoke screen for the 1st Guards Army which was counterattacking towards Gumrak. This meant that the Il-2s had to fly at extremely low level through heavy flak – regimental CO, Maj K V Yarovoy, led the group. Although the mission was a success, and Soviet infantry dislodged the enemy, Yarovoy was shot down and killed.

Attack aircraft also participated in the battle for the central and southern parts of Stalingrad, flying 57 per cent of all combat sorties during this phase in the defence of the beleaguered Soviet city. Those missions flown over the centre of Stalingrad itself proved to be especially demanding, for pilots had to search through a maze of demolished buildings as they hunted for enemy weapon emplacements in specific streets and houses, prior to destroying them. Eight Il-2s from 504th ShAP, led by Snr Lt Pstygo, were among the first to open their account in this street fighting when they attacked enemy tanks on the western edge of the Krasniy Oktyabr Factory on 17 September.

Five groups of Il-2s from 206th and 226th ShAD, escorted by fighters from 268th and 288th IAD, combed the streets on 20 September. At 0645 hrs, eight Il-2s from 504th ShAP, led by the regimental navigator, Capt Prutkov, attacked tanks and personnel carriers near Aviagorodok and the Central Airfield. Seven 505th ShAP Il-2s led by Maj Vasiliev, who was also a regimental navigator, hit Aviagorodok again at 1010 hrs.

A third group of eight Il-2s, led by Snr Lt Pstygo, attacked enemy tanks and vehicles near the railway station, in the main square and in Kommunisticheskaya and Saratovskaya streets at 1300 hrs. Six aircraft from 607th ShAP, headed by squadron leader Snr Lt Lobanov, attacked infantry along the railway tracks and north of the station. Finally, a fifth group of six Il-2s from 504th and 944th ShAPs, escorted by ten LaGG-3s from 296th IAP and led by squadron leader Maj Eremin, attacked tanks and mechanised infantry 2.5 km (1.5 miles) southwest of Malakhov Kurgan.

These strikes were particularly effective, and were appreciated by 62nd Army's commander, Gen Chuykov, as well as by Gen Khryukin. For his part in the operation, Snr Lt Pstygo was promoted to captain and recommended for a decoration. His wingman, Sgt Vedenin, received the Order of the Red Banner and was also promoted. A malfunctioning engine had delayed Vedenin, forcing him to make a solo attack without escorts.

Although flying near-constant patrols over Stalingrad, the Il-2s failed to stop German forces from

Outstanding combat survivability was a key feature of the Il-2. The armour protection often saved pilots from injury when hit by flak or attacked by fighters. In this case, the damage to the side of the Il-2's cockpit has been caused by two MG 151 20 mm cannon rounds fired by a German aircraft

Four single-seat Il-2s prepare to fall into line astern formation prior to commencing their attack run on the target

reaching the industrial area of the city on 27 September. A week later they launched assaults on the Stalingrad Tractor Factory, as well as the Barrikady and Krasniy Oktyabr factories. These assaults would continue until 18 November.

To reduce losses to German fighters and flak during this period, Il-2s often flew at dusk and dawn, as well during moonlit nights. From 28 August until 18 November, *Shturmovik* units undertook 406 such sorties, attacking airfields, railway junctions and trains. Such targets were relatively easy to detect at night, and on some occasions Polikarpov U-2 biplane trainers were pressed into service as pathfinders, detecting and illuminating targets by dropping flares and incendiary bombs a few minutes ahead of the Il-2s. In one such operation on the night of 24 October, 19 pilots from 228th ShAD, together with ten U-2s from 271st NBAD, made a highly effective attack on German troops 30 km (19 miles) northwest of Stalingrad. Working in relays throughout the mission, specially-assigned U-2s designated the targets for the Il-2s and other Polikarpov biplanes.

With a shortage of fighters, and flak guns being used in an anti-tank role to fend off marauding panzers, the Soviets relied on Il-2s to intercept German Ju 87, Ju 88 and He 111 bombers during the latter stages of the defence of Stalingrad. On 11 October, 505th ShAP CO Maj Chumachenko, together with his wingman, intercepted 12 unescorted Ju 88s near Elton station. One bomber sustained heavy damage from rockets and machine gun fire and made an emergency landing near 500th ShAP's base. After a short firefight with soldiers from Snr Lt Toropov's signals company, the German bomber crew were captured.

Four days later, at 1600 hrs, 225th ShAP squadron leader Snr Lt Tyulenev, together with his wingman, were guided onto an He 111 bomber flying at an altitude of 1000 m (3000 ft) by a ground radio operator. The Soviet attack aircraft launched their rockets and then fired their guns at the Heinkel, which crashed and exploded near the village of Blagodarniy. Soon afterwards, the pair encountered two more He 111s and engaged them at a range of 100-150 m (120-180 yrd). One of the German aircraft crashed and exploded near the village of Novonikolskoe.

On 22 October, Sgt Sudarkin of 945th ShAP engaged five He 111s attempting to bomb a train carrying a tank unit as it sat stationary in Shungai station. He succeeded in downing one of the Heinkels and forcing the others to jettison their bombs and make a run for it. 206th ShAD's CO, Col Sryvkin, promoted Sudarkin upon his return to base.

Despite the adverse environment, Red Army units offered stiff resistance to the German troops. The Don Front went on the offensive on 19 October, and 64th Army dealt a powerful blow to the German flank outside the city six days later, halting the assault. A 206th ShAD situation report issued that very day described 64th Army's counter-attack;

'Divisional aircraft, escorted by fighters from 268th IAD, attacked enemy tanks, vehicles, infantry, artillery and weapon emplacements in the suburbs of Minin, Sadovaya, Verkhnyaya Elshanka, Peschanka, Peschaniy ravine and the northern edge of the forest west of Elshanka and Spartakovskaya. A total of 43 Il-2s flew 90 combat sorties, two of which failed to fulfil their combat mission due to malfunctions and five more due to their failure to rendezvous with escort fighters.

This German motorised convoy was devastated by Il-2s as it approached Ordzhonikidze in late 1942

The Il-2's outstanding survivability often enabled pilots to carry out a successful emergency landing on any more or less suitable ground, or to reach their home base and land there safely. A groundcrewman can be seen checking the extent of the underwing damage suffered by this battle-scarred *Shturmovik*

'The intensity of enemy air defence artillery fire increased considerably later in the day, and patrols of three to four Bf 109s appeared over the target. The Germans opened a dense barrage near the Mokraya Mechetka River and along the Volga River.'

A total of six groups of five to six Il-2s from 686th, 807th, and 945th ShAP had flown combat sorties that day. They destroyed or damaged up to 11 tanks, 20 vehicles, 17 carts laden with cargo, two weapon emplacements and a field artillery battery. Their losses included an Il-2 piloted by MSgt Sudarkin from 945th ShAP. The wing of his aircraft was hit by two anti-aircraft shells and he was then attacked by a Messerschmitt. The engine in his aircraft seized as it limped over the Volga, forcing Sudarkin to make a belly-landing five kilometres (three miles) south of Prishchevka.

The following day, aircraft from 206th ShAD, escorted by fighters from 268th IAD, attacked tanks, vehicles, carts, artillery and infantry in ravines near Sadovaya and Elshanka. They destroyed and damaged up to 12 tanks, 29 vehicles, ten carts, five guns and a field artillery battery. Sgt Malyshev was killed when his burning aircraft crashed on Sarpinskiy Island. Four other Il-2s were heavily damaged by flak.

On the 27th, 206th ShAD's 27 attack aircraft regiments flew 42 combat sorties over the city streets. Returning crews reported heavy anti-aircraft artillery fire and patrols of six to eight Bf 109s over the target area. Lacking the promised support of escort fighters from 268th IAD, the unit suffered considerable losses as a result. That day, 945th ShAP alone conducted 26 combat sorties and lost three Il-2s, with four more damaged. Capt Vanifatiev and Sgts Pozdnyakov and Prokhorenko were killed, and Lt Makarov's aircraft took a direct hit from anti-aircraft artillery while attacking German troops in Lenin Street. Although its wing, landing gear and controls were damaged Makarov managed to make it back to his base, where he spent 30 minutes trying to extend the Il-2's undercarriage. He had been ordered to belly-land the aircraft, but his persistence was rewarded when the undercarriage finally extended and Makarov was able to land conventionally. His aircraft was repaired and ready for action several hours later.

Later that same day, Luftwaffe fighters hit Lt Mironov's Il-2 during a strike on a concentration of mechanised infantry near Elshanka. The aircraft's controls and landing gear were damaged, while Mironov was wounded in the arm and the right

Hero of the Battle of Stalingrad and future twice a HSU, Lt M G Gareev of 76th GShAP is seen here at Kotelnikovo airfield in April-May 1943. After the battle for the city on the Volga, the People's Commissar of Defence ordered 226th ShAD to be transformed into 1st Guards Attack Aircraft Division on 18 March 1943. The division's regiments received the Guards title as well, 504th ShAP becoming 74th GShAP, 505th ShAP being redesignated 75th GShAP and 225th ShAP 76th GShAP

side. Bleeding profusely, he managed to fly home and land his aircraft. Mironov received the Order of the Red Banner.

COUNTER-OFFENSIVE

Supreme High Command General Headquarters adopted a plan for a major counter-offensive on 13 November involving the 17th, 16th, and 8th Air Armies. The attack force included seven air divisions (206th, 214th, 289th, 291st, 228th, 267th and 227th) and two independent air regiments (208th and 637th), equipped with a total of 317 operational and 133 unserviceable Il-2s.

Despite bad weather, the attack aircraft pilots fulfilled every mission tasking asked of them, providing efficient close air support to friendly ground troops. Soviet forces encircled the Sixth Field Army and units of 4th Panzer Army outside the city, leaving the enemy with little option but to keep these trapped units supplied with ammunition, fuel, food and medicines brought in by air. Bombers were pressed into service alongside military transports. Soviet fighters and attack aircraft did their best to hamper this operation during the day by bombing and strafing key airfields. U-2 nuisance bombers took over this task after dark, remaining on station to drop their bombs as soon as the runway lights were lit.

Despite the steps taken by the VVS RKKA command, there were still instances of a lack of coordination between escorting fighters and the aircraft they were supposed to protect. The Luftwaffe fighter pilots, who were still operating extremely effectively, took full advantage of such situations whenever they arose. An attack on Pitomnik airfield by Capt Emelyanov's pilots from 622nd ShAP on 10 December was one such mission to end in tragedy. According to the regimental combat log, only three of seven Il-2s despatched returned from the mission. It noted;

'A group led by Jnr Lt Opalev did not return from the combat mission for unknown reasons. The same holds true for Jnr Lt Goryachev and air gunner Razumnov from Karpov's group. Aircraft piloted by Mordavtsev and Dogalev were hit.'

It transpired that four La-5s from 13th IAP were unable to provide the Il-2s with reliable protection, leaving Opalev's group exposed to highly effective and battle-hardened German fighter pilots. The entire group was shot down, with the first to fall being the aircraft piloted by Sgt Dolberidze. Attacked over the frontline by four Bf 109s, the pilot had to make an emergency landing in Soviet-held territory. The Il-2s of Kuznetsov and Opalev were hit near Pitomnik airfield, with both pilots crash-landing in no man's land near German positions. They were only saved by the swift action of a Red Army company supported by two tanks.

The squadron political officer, Capt Artemiev, who was acting as Sgt Kuznetsov's air gunner, shot down a Bf 109 during a dogfight with the enemy fighters, while Jnr Lt Opalev managed to destroy another Messerschmitt by carrying out the most effective manoeuvre open to attack aircraft in such situations. When a pair of Bf 109s closed in, he suddenly throttled back and machine-gunned the leading German fighter as it flew past him. The Messerschmitt started billowing smoke and crashed near Pitomnik airfield.

Despite the enemy's intervention, Kuznetsov and Opalev made two attack runs on the German base, leaving a number of aircraft ablaze.

Exactly a month later, *Shturmovik* pilots from 622nd ShAP were able to avenge their fallen comrades. On 9 January 1943, seven Il-2s, led by Capt Bakhtin and escorted by seven Yak-1s from 236th IAP, bombed Salsk airfield. The attack was so effective that it was subsequently included in textbooks on attack aviation tactics.

This snow-camouflaged Il-2 of 504th ShAP (74th GShAP from 18 March 1943) was assigned to Snr Lt A I Borodin, who, by decree of the USSR Supreme Council, was awarded the title of HSU for his part in combat operations over the River Volga in 1942-43

When the Red Army reached Tatsinskaya and Morozovsk, Salsk airfield had become the main German aerial re-supply base – aerial reconnaissance revealed the presence of up to 150 aircraft of various types. The Il-2s made their first run over the target after diving from cloud cover, bombing and strafing German aircraft on the ground for 15 minutes from 1108 hrs to 1123 hrs. They expended a total of 26 FAB-100 bombs and 56 RS-82 rockets, together with 1386 VYa, 300 ShVAK, 120 UBT and 3820 ShKAS cannon and machine gun rounds. The anti-aircraft gunners failed to open fire until the Soviet attack aircraft had made their first pass.

While the Il-2s attacked enemy aircraft on the ground, their escort fighters engaged four Bf 109s as the *Shturmoviks* made good their escape. However, a second group of Messerschmitts attacked the Il-2s as they headed for home, and the Soviet air gunners managed to shoot down two of them, with a third falling to the Yak-1s during the initial dogfight over the target area. Soviet losses amounted to two Il-2s, which were downed by flak over enemy territory, and two Yak-1s lost in aerial engagements.

German losses were considerably higher, with a post-mission photo-reconnaissance flight returning with imagery which revealed that as many as 72 Ju 52/3m transport aircraft had been destroyed or damaged at Salsk airfield. This was, however, an exceptionally successful attack, as the average Il-2 strike usually inflicted considerably less damage on the enemy. Even taking into account the tendency for attacking crews to exaggerate enemy losses, the results achieved by Capt Bakhtin's group on 9 January were impressive – at least two to three enemy aircraft destroyed or damaged for each flight crew participating in the mission.

ATTACKING TRANSPORT AIRCRAFT

The targeting of German transport aircraft by VVS RKKA was to yield outstanding results. According to the air armies and the headquarters of the Don and Stalingrad Fronts, this two-month offensive resulted in the destruction or damage beyond repair of 1057 transport aircraft and bombers. Of this number, 467 were downed on their way to or from the besieged city. However, the most significant result for the Red Army was that soldiers of the encircled Sixth Army received an average of 80-100 tons of cargo a day instead of the required daily minimum of 600 tons.

Army Group Don, under Generalfeldmarschall Erich von Manstein, attempted a breakthrough from the Kotelnikovo area on 12 December 1942. Von Manstein planned to overrun the outer positions manned by Gen Trufanov's encircling 51st Army and rescue Generaloberst Friedrich Paulus' Sixth Army in the city itself.

Il-2 units were badly affected by adverse weather during this period, with flight crews having to contend with heavy snow and poor visibility. Often, they had to fly without fighter escorts. In view of the poor weather, and the heavy losses being suffered by *Shturmovik* units, Gen Khryukin ordered 206th ShAD to assemble a task force comprising the ten most combat-ready flight crews from 503rd, 686th, 811th and 945th ShAPs, together with six pilots from 226th ShAD. The force was to be led by 206th ShAD's deputy CO, Lt Col Chumachenko.

The task force flew its first mission on 18 December, when six Il-2s from 686th ShAP, led by squadron leader Slobodnichenko, bombed German tanks and vehicles reported to be hiding in gullies two kilometres (1.25 miles) south of Leskina and Neklinskaya. The escorting fighters from 268th IAD lost sight of the group in heavy cloud, and the Il-2s were quickly set upon by four German fighters while recovering from the attack. All the Il-2s were shot down in the ensuing dogfight, with two pilots making emergency landings near the village of Verkhne-Kumskiy, which had been secured by the Soviet 59th Armour Brigade literally hours earlier. The fate of the other pilots is unknown.

The following day, pilots from the combined assault task force had two noteworthy aerial engagements with German bombers. In the first combat sortie, four Il-2s from 503rd and 945th ShAPs, escorted by six Yak-1s, encountered six Ju 87s over Kosh between them and the target. The Il-2s attacked the Stukas and shot one down, before carrying on with their assigned mission by attacking German forces in the Neklinskaya gully and the ravines north of Klykov. They destroyed or damaged two tanks and three vehicles.

In the second sortie, five Il-2s from 686th and 811th ShAPs ran into a formation of six Ju 87s and eight Bf 109Fs after their attack. The Soviet aircraft shot down three Stukas during the ensuing brief dog-fight without loss.

The tension in the frontline amongst the Il-2 units involved in what has become known as the Battle of Stalingrad is well illustrated by the following order issued from 206th ShAD headquarters on 19 December 1942;

'The enemy has concentrated 240 tanks and infantry in the area of collective farms 8 Marta, Verkhne-Kumskiy, the southern end of the Kumskaya gully and Zagotskot. 206th ShAD commander orders 807th, and 503rd ShAP, and attached crews from 945th ShAP, escorted by 296th IAP, to destroy enemy tanks, mechanised infantry and artillery in the area. The Front Military Council and 8th Air Army Commander demand that the enemy penetrating forces be destroyed on 20 December 1942. Attack aviation is to carry out as many run-ins on the target as possible, and achieve the greatest efficiency.'

Despite cloud cover down to 250-300 m (800-1000 ft) and poor visibility, 8th Air Army generated 393 combat sorties on 20 December in response to the order – this was the greatest number flown in a single day throughout the whole Stalingrad Front operation. This achievement was to be overshadowed by a serious friendly fire incident, however. A flight from 503rd ShAP, led by Capt Demekhin, lost its bearings and attacked friendly forces near Verkhne-Tsaritsynskiy. The Il-2s bombed and strafed 20th Anti-Tank Artillery Brigade of 2nd Guards Army reserves.

Subsequent investigation showed
that the group leader had lost his
bearings and 503rd ShAP's commander had also failed to ensure
that the group leader and his group
were fully briefed. Both were judged
to blame for this failure. As a result,
Demekhin was summoned before
the Military Tribunal, while the
503rd ShAP CO was relieved of his
duties. However, by decree of the
Presidium of the USSR Supreme
Council, dated 13 April 1944,
Demekhin was awarded the title of
HSU for his combat feats.

The *Yaroslavskiy Komsomolets*
squadron had its Il-2 attack aircraft
was paid for by Yaroslavl Komsomol
members (three of whom are seen
here conversing with a *Shturmovik*
pilot). These suitably marked aircraft
were handed over to 667th ShAP
(141st GShAP from 5 March 1944)
in January 1943

Army Group Don failed to capitalise on the successes it had achieved
at the beginning of the operation it had launched on 12 December, and
eventually German troops were forced to retreat in the face of a fierce
counterattack mounted by 2nd Guards Army and 51st Army on
24 December. Kotelnikovo was liberated by Soviet forces on the morning
of the 29th, and Soviet troops crossed the Don and captured Tormosin
the following day. The German advance had finally grounded to a halt.

By early January 1943, the Soviet side had created the right conditions
for Operation *Koltso* (Ring) to be launched. This offensive was intended
to finally destroy the encircled German troops under von Paulus'
command. The Don Front went on the offensive as early as the 10th,
when Soviet forces overran the German defensive lines and destroyed the
last remaining combat unit in northern Stalingrad on 2 February. The
Battle of Stalingrad was over.

The Red Army's next task was to drive the Germans from the
Caucasus. Offensive operations were mounted near Voronezh, Velikie
Luki and Rzhev, as well as between the rivers Don and Oskol. As a result,
Soviet forces were able to liberate a significant amount of territory, and
with it cities like Kharkov, Belgorod, Velikie Luki and Rzhev. German
forces suffered heavy losses in both manpower and equipment as they
hastily retreated westward.

By order of the People's Commissar of Defence, dated 18 March 1943,
226th and 228th ShADs, which had particularly distinguished

The remains of a German Ju 86K
reconnaissance aircraft shot down
by Snr Lt V B Emelyanenko over
Kagarlitskaya railway station on
9 January 1943. Il-2s operated as
makeshift fighters on numerous
occasions in 1942-43

themselves in the Battle of Stalingrad, were transformed into 1st and
2nd GShADs, respectively. Under
the same order, 243rd ShAD, which
had fought in the North-Western
Front, became 3rd GShAD. Six
weeks later, the People's Commissar
of Defence issued an order (on
1 May 1943) transforming 212th
and 267th ShADs, which had
fought extraordinarily well at
Velikie Luki and Rzhev into 4th and
5th GShADs, respectively.

THE TIDE TURNS

By the spring of 1943, the heaviest fighting of the Great Patriotic War was taking place in the central part of the Soviet-German Front. Taking advantage of mistakes made by the Soviet command, the Germans had launched a powerful counter-offensive against the Voronezh Front. From their starting point near Lyubotin, German forces had recaptured Kharkov on 16 March and seized Belgorod two days later, but they were unable to advance any further north. With the Kursk front now stabilised, both sides prepared themselves for the decisive battle of the war on the eastern front.

The German command planned two powerful thrusts in the general direction of Kursk from south of Orel and north of Kharkov. Their objective was to encircle and destroy the Central and Voronezh Fronts defending the Kursk salient. Success would gain them manoeuvring room to seize the shortest route to Moscow.

The Supreme High Command General Headquarters became aware of the planned German summer offensive just in time, and as early as 12 April it was decided to wear the enemy down by resorting to active defence in depth, thus forcing the Germans to commit their reserves and destroy them in a counterattack. Soviet planners concluded that they would have to rely on a massive deployment of tanks and aircraft, since their infantry had been exhausted defended Stalingrad, reducing it in strength to a shadow of its former self.

It was on this basis that Soviet air power was directed against the central and adjacent parts of the German front between 6 and 16 May. The ultimate goal was to destroy German aircraft on the ground and in the air, as well as to target road and rail transport. Soviet planners aimed to disrupt enemy preparations for the forthcoming battles and achieve air superiority from the outset of the German offensive. The operation was expected to involve tactical aviation units of the Western, Bryansk, Central, Voronezh, South-Western and Southern Fronts, with the major burden of combat operations falling on the Il-2s of 1st and 2nd GShADs and 224th, 233rd, 266th, 292nd, 290th and 299th ShADs.

Historians have long considered that the tactical aviation units involved in this large-scale campaign flew both decisively and effectively during operations in May 1943. A closer look at the statistics from this period reveal that this was not quite the case, however, for the losses suffered by Soviet air armies during a series of strikes on enemy airfields flown on 6-7 May alone

'Half a wing and a sheer miracle' – that is what pilots used to say about the Il-2's survivability. Despite sustaining severe combat damage inflicted by several well-aimed heavy-calibre flak bursts, this aircraft from 7th GShAP managed to return from a mission during the summer of 1943

Il-2 construction number 301740 of 820th ShAP (155th GShAP from 5 February 1944) suffered heavy damage when it was hit by a flak shell during the attack on Kharkov-Sokolniki airfield on 6 May 1943. Its pilot, L Ostrov, nevertheless managed to reach his home base and land his aircraft safely, and the Il-2 was quickly repaired and returned to operational status

Il-2s from 7th GShAP head for German positions in loose formation on the North Caucasus Front in August 1943

resulted in the destruction of 70 Il-2s. According to regimental headquarters, nine were shot down by Luftwaffe fighters, eight by anti-aircraft artillery, 36 did not return from missions and 17 were scrapped after making emergency landings.

The toll of personnel was no less high, with 52 pilots and 41 air gunners failing to return – pilots having little or no combat experience in Il-2s accounted for 52 per cent of all losses. The remaining 48 per cent were seasoned veterans, and of these, 21 per cent were COs (regimental commanders and navigators, as well as squadron and flight leaders), while the other 27 per cent were experienced senior pilots. It also has to be admitted that the Soviet air armies failed to destroy the number of aircraft on airfields as demanded by the Supreme High Command General HQ. Therefore, the operation's objective was not achieved.

The fact was that these heavy losses, and the overall lack of effectiveness of the Soviet strikes, was due to deficiencies in the work of unit HQs at all levels. Orders did not always take into account such vital factors as the operational environment, target defences and combat capabilities of the Il-2 units themselves. There was also a lack of cooperation among the various aviation arms. Missions were not properly briefed, and Soviet fighters once again showed their inability to defend Il-2s from German fighters. As a result, entire Il-2 groups were lost attacking enemy airfields.

On 6 May, for example, 16 Il-2s from 41st ShAP, 299th ShAD set out, but only one crew (Capt Fedorov and air gunner Isaev) returned. Even then, both men were seriously wounded and their aircraft peppered with numerous shell holes. Two more flight crews were found after a search.

Fedorov reported that while approaching the Orel-GVF airfield, heavy flak had been encountered – German flak guns were sited around the outskirts of the city, and they also ringed the airfield. The Il-2 groups became strung out after the attack as the wingmen, most of whom were novice pilots, were unable to stay in formation. And when the leaders throttled back to allow the stragglers to catch up, German fighters pounced. The Il-2s failed to form a defensive formation, and the engagement became a chaotic free-for-all. Fedorov said he had not seen any Soviet fighters in the target area.

Subsequent investigation showed that, contrary to standing orders, two groups of eight Yak-1 escort fighters from 896th IAP, 286th IAD had flown well above 1000-

1200 m (3250-4000 ft), some 800 m (700 yrd) behind the Il-2s. They had climbed even higher when German flak gunners opened up, with the result that they lost sight of their charges during the *Shturmoviks'* attacks.

A group of 12 Il-2s from 58th and 79th GShAPs, 2nd GShAD struck Khmelevaya airfield on 7 May, and again only one crew survived. Their machine was written off when Capt Parshin and gunner Snr Sgt Matveev were forced to crash near Novosil after being shot up by enemy fighters.

A study of the archives reveals the chain of events leading up to this disaster. Even before they had reached the target, both groups of attack aircraft, together with escort fighters from 176th and 563rd IAPs, 283rd IAD, had encountered heavy flak near Kroma. A defensive manoeuvre resulted in the general combat formation breaking up, with the fighter pilots panicking and heady for nearby clouds in an effort to escape the highly accurate anti-aircraft fire. The flak also caused both groups of Il-2s to lose their bearings and miss Khmelevaya airfield altogether.

Six *Shturmoviks* from 79th GShAP, led by Capt Parshin, duly found themselves near Karachev, while another group of six aircraft from 58th GShAP, led by Lt Mingalev, reached Naryshkino. On pinpointing his location, Mingalev decided to attack the nearest airfield, Orel-Tsentralniy, while Parshin led his group back to Khmelevaya, which had been their original target. While the attack aircraft were wandering around unescorted over enemy territory, ten fighters from 519th IAP had found the German airfield at Khomuty. When the Il-2s had not appeared after several minutes, however, the fighters headed for home.

Elsewhere, 79th GShAP Il-2s were attacked by up to 12 Fw 190s as they approached Khmelevaya. They also encountered flak, splitting the group up prior to the Il-2s commencing their attack. The aircraft became even more strung-out after they had completed their attack runs, which meant that they failed to reform in a tight formation. Instead, they retreated in pairs or independently, thus ruling out any possibility of the crews adopting a defensive formation should they be attacked by enemy fighters. And sure enough, each Il-2 was set upon by up to four Fw 190s, which made simultaneous firing passes from various directions.

Parshin and his air gunner Matveev downed a Focke-Wulf fighter, but the remaining aircraft chased their Il-2 as it fled east over Sheremetievka.

This Il-2 of 820th ShAP, flown by Sgt Zakharov, was also damaged during the regiment's attack on German-held Kharkov-Sokolniki airfield on 6 May 1943. While withdrawing from the target, Zakharov was attacked by two Bf 109s and his *Shturmovik* badly shot up. Zakharov and his air gunner, Sgt Belokonniy, were both slightly wounded, although this did not stop the latter from taking his revenge by shooting down one of the German fighters with an accurate burst of machine-gun fire

Here, Matveev destroyed another Fw 190 in a head-on attack, before crashing near Novosil. He had no knowledge of what had happened to the rest of his group when questioned by his superiors.

It was a similar story when Il-2s from 58th GShAP attacked Orel-Tsentralniy airfield, as anti-aircraft guns sited there, and around the south-western outskirts of Orel, engaged the *Shturmoviks* as they approached. Yak-1 escort fighters from 176th IAP dispersed in ones and twos and plunged into the clouds, leaving the Il-2s to press on

53

alone. When the latter began their withdrawal, the flak stopped and 12 Fw 190s appeared from the north and attacked the unescorted Il-2s.

In his combat report of 7 May, 58th GShAP CO and HSU, Capt V M Golubev, said that none of the fighter pilots involved could explain what had happened over Orel-Tsentralniy after they had been dispersed by flak. Although the Yak-1s escaped unscathed, the Il-2s, which had failed to establish a suitable formation, had all fallen victim to enemy fighters.

Those combat sorties that had been properly organised and prepared yielded good results, including the strike delivered by aircraft from 673rd ShAP, 266th ShAD on Rogan airfield on 6 May. During preparations for this mission, crews were able to study reconnaissance photos of the airfield taken at 1755 hrs the previous day. These images revealed that there were no fewer than 107 Bf 109s and Fw 190s on the airfield.

With this information to hand, the regimental CO, Capt Matnakov, was able to thoroughly brief the flight crews involved. He specified the manoeuvres each crew was to make, how they would withdraw from the target area and where they would rendezvous.

The route to the target was chosen to enable the Il-2s to cross the frontline in a remote area and allow them to keep clear of enemy VNOS (*Vozdoushnoe Nablyudenie, Opoveshchenie i Svyaz* – Air Observation, Warning, and Communications) posts and air defence artillery positions.

The first wave of Il-2s, led by Capt Eliseev, took off at 0443 hrs and was followed two minutes later by the second, headed by Jnr Lt Aleksandrov. Despite the darkness, and fog and haze, both groups took off and joined up almost perfectly. They met 18 La-5s from 240th and 193rd IAPs, 302nd IAD over Urazovo fighter base. About 12 kilometres (7.5 miles) from Rogan airfield, the Il-2 pilots throttled their engines back to reduce noise and glided down to an altitude of 1150 m (3750 ft) as they positioned themselves to attack from out of the rising sun.

It was 0520 hrs when the first two *Shturmoviks* raced over the German base, targeting aircraft positioned on the western and southern edges of the airfield. Each pair of Il-2s initially attacked with rockets and gunfire, before dropping bombs from an altitude of 400-600 m (1300-2000 ft). They then turned their attention to the flak guns, as well as any German aircraft that still appeared to be intact. After the mission, the Il-2s joined up over the Mokhnachi forest and headed home in tight formation.

The German defensive fire had been rather weak, unorganised and – because the gunners had the sun in their eyes – inaccurate. Even so, three Il-2s were slightly damaged by flak. Attacking pilots claimed to have destroyed or damaged up to 30 aircraft, started 18 fires and suppressed eight flak emplacements. Photo-reconnaissance of Rogan airfield later showed that Luftwaffe losses probably amounted to six fighters in total – not a bad result, especially as no Il-2s had been lost.

TRANSPORT TARGETS

From 6 May, a ten-day sequence of strikes on rail and road traffic was

Not all Il-2s made it back to base, however. This unidentified *Shturmovik* crash-landed in German-held territory in the spring of 1943. Laying on his back on the Il-2's holed wing, one of its crewmen appears to have either died of his wounds or been shot by German troops as he tried to flee from the downed attack aircraft launched. Several months earlier, on 26 January, in fact, a pair of Il-2s from 7th GShAP, piloted by Lt Smirnov and Jnr Lt Slepov, had attacked a key railway station and shown what could be achieved, even by a small force. Searching for targets in the Stavropol, Tikhoretsk and Kavkazskaya areas in bad weather, the pilots found and attacked four troop trains at Malorossiyskaya station. A series of deafening explosions rocked the trains and a fierce fire broke out that produced such thick acrid smoke that the station itself was obscured from view.

The success of this attack was confirmed by a special 4th Air Army commission, which inspected the station when the area was liberated. It was determined that the pilots had indeed destroyed all four trains. One had been carrying fuel, another tanks and the remaining two ammunition. The tracks themselves had been so badly damaged that the Germans had been unable to repair them – not one troop train had left for Tikhoretsk in four days. There had been much disruption as a result, and many stranded trains were captured by the Red Army.

The Soviet Supreme Commander-in-Chief, Joseph Stalin himself, had held up the attack by Smirnov and Slepov as an example to the entire Red Army Air Force in an order dated 4 May 1943. Stalin also demanded that 'The Soviet Air Force is to assign priority to delivering air strikes against railway trains, attacking enemy motor convoys and hunting down vehicles in the enemy's rear so as to disrupt enemy traffic'.

By the time Stalin had singled their action out for rare praise, Slepov had been killed in action and Smirnov captured after his aircraft was hit by anti-aircraft fire – he had tried to cross the frontline but crash-landed in German-held territory and was taken prisoner. Confined to several concentration camps, Smirnov managed to escape to fight with a partisan unit in Czechoslovakia. As a result, neither Slepov nor Smirnov were decorated for their attack on Malorossiyskaya station.

In compliance with Stalin's order, each air army allocated an attack aircraft regiment and a fighter regiment to anti-supply route operations, with the units concerned being ordered to 'free-hunt' in small groups.

During one of the very first such missions to be flown, a pair of Il-2s from 617th ShAP, 291st ShAD, comprising squadron leader Lt Proshkin (air gunner MSgt Sapiev) and flight leader Jnr Lt Aleksukhin (air gunner Jnr Sgt Apukhin), took off at 0437 hrs on 7 May for a free-hunt along the Sumy-Belopolie railway line. The Il-2s flew at an altitude of 3000-5000 m (10,000-16,000ft) along a route plotted in advance, crossing the frontline over a forest and then hugging the ground as far away from populated areas as possible. At 0500 hrs they sighted a train and 42 goods wagons chocked full of troops approaching Ambary station.

The Il-2s initially attacked the locomotive in a 30-degree dive from a height of 100-120 m (300-400 ft) at a range of 2000-3000 m from the train, Proshkin dropping FAB-50

This German locomotive pulling goods wagons filled with troops was damaged by Soviet attack aircraft at Shklov station

Jnr Lt V P Aleksukhin and his air gunner, A D Gatayunov, formed the most successful flight crew of 617th ShAP (167th GShAP from 5 April, 1944) in 1943-44. Credited with attacking literally dozens of trains, they are seen here about to undertake yet another a combat mission in the Kharkov sector in August 1943

This was the kind of destruction Jnr Lt V P Aleksukhin and his comrades inflicted on German troop trains during the spring and summer of 1943

bombs on the engine while his wingman Aleksukhin strafed it. Enveloped in smoke, the locomotive stopped. Aleksukhin then dropped his FAB-50s on the goods wagons during his second pass, while Proshkin launched his rockets at the flak guns mounted on platform cars – he also raked them with machine gun fire. Six follow-up attacks on the train met no resistance. In addition to the locomotive, the pilots damaged 30 goods wagons and set some of them alight.

The following morning the same crews, 'free-hunting' along the Zolochev-Gotnya railway line, detected a 50-wagon train (30 goods wagons, ten platform cars and ten tank cars) three kilometres from Zolochev station at 0510 hrs. Proshkin initially suppressed the fire from light flak guns mounted on platform cars during his first attack run. Aleksukhin, flying 300-400 m behind his leader, simultaneously bombed the head of the train. The pilots made five more runs apiece, scoring direct hits on the engine with their rockets, setting two goods wagons alight and destroying cargo on the platform cars. The train eventually broke into two parts, with the tail section rolling down a slope towards Zolochev. Both Il-2s were damaged by light flak.

On the night of 8 May, Proshkin and Aleksukhin set out on yet another free-hunt that took them south of Gotnya, Graivoron and Bolshaya Piskarevka. Taking off at 1930 hrs, they again approached the frontline at low-level and then climbed a little higher once the sun had fully set. Both pilots then spent 30 minutes searching for a suitable target prior to detecting 70+ vehicles near Graivoron. They lined up on their targets at a distance of five kilometres (three miles) and strafed two trucks, but it was too dark to see the results of their initial attack.

Proshkin and Aleksukhin then made four more runs each, launching rockets and firing their cannon and machine guns in their first pass, dropping their bombs and strafing the targets in the second and using their guns in the follow-up attacks. They later reported that the target area had been enveloped in such thick smoke after the second run that they had barely been able to discern the enemy vehicles. Although the target was protected by light anti-aircraft artillery, the Il-2s sustained insignificant damage.

On 9 May, 299th ShAP, 290th ShAD assigned three pairs of Il-2s (led by Capt Sotnikov and Jnr Lts Ivanov and Obukhov) to hunt for trains in the Barvenkovo-Lozovaya and Lozovaya-Belyaevka areas. The pilots destroyed five locomotives, burnt-out a troop train and set an additional ten goods wagons alight. They also attacked a convoy on the move and wrecked five vehicles.

In the early hours of 12 May, four Il-2s from the same regiment (led by Jnr Lts Zheleznyakov and Obukhov) attacked and destroyed six vehicles near Brazhkovka. While they were recovering from the attack, the Soviet aircraft were intercepted by four Bf 109s – two attacked Zheleznyakov's pair and the other two Obukhov's. The German pilots managed to isolate Obukhov during the dogfight, and the other Il-2 crews lost sight of him. Obukhov and his air gunner, Jnr Sgt Gubin, did not return.

That same day, Sgts N Smirnov and A Smirnov from 6th GShAP, 3rd Air Army struck two trains at Vlasie junction. Attacking 'out of the sun', their three passes left the locomotive damaged and destroyed two carriages and two platform trucks carrying vehicles. After the sergeants had landed and been debriefed, another group of four Il-2s, headed by Snr Lt Feofanov, was sent to finish off the job. They in turn managed to damage six goods wagons and seven platform trucks carrying vehicles.

Subsequent events were to show that these operations had attained their objective of disrupting enemy road and rail traffic. As a direct result of this campaign, the build up of German forces in the Kursk salient had been slowed, allowing Red Army units to defend the area. But these successes in turn meant that VVS RKKA and air army commands failed to appreciate the seriousness of the losses suffered by Il-2 units in May.

Measures to improve mission organisation and cooperation between fighters and Il-2s did not take priority during training, and these were the very reasons why the air armies were to suffer near-catastrophic losses in personnel and equipment in the Kursk area during July and August. As if to further reinforce this point, in mid-June 1943, Red Army General Staff officer Maj Kuzmichev, assigned to 2nd Air Army HQ, reported to Marshal Vasilevskiy that, given the existing command and control system, 'the efficiency of the aviation command and control would not be maintained, especially during massive strikes and manoeuvres'.

During their planning for the Battle of Kursk (codenamed Operation *Citadel* by the Germans), the *Wehrmacht* must have taken into account the swollen command, control and communications (C3) system displayed by VVS RKKA and the Red Army, as well as the fact that 'once disrupted, the Russian Air Force's ground-based C3 system cannot be quickly restored'. A disruption of the C3 system, and of the liaison between ground troops and aviation on the battlefield, would significantly undermine Soviet defences, despite the communists boasting numerical superiority. The disintegration of the C3 system would hand the advantage to the enemy.

This, in fact, is exactly what happened. The Soviet command could not properly respond to the rapid

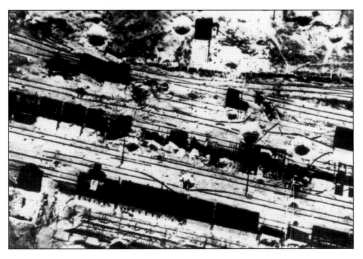

An aerial photo-reconnaissance view of yet another German marshalling yard devastated by Il-2s during the Kursk campaign

57

changes that characterised the opening phases of the Battle of Kursk. The Germans launched a massive and highly dynamic offensive which combined air power, army air defence systems and armoured units concentrated within a narrow part of the front. As a result, the enemy was able to seize the initiative.

As Red Army General Staff officer Maj Kuzmichev had feared, the plans of the Soviet air armies in response to the German assault did

not correspond to battlefield reality. Squadron-size Il-2 air strikes were too small to be effective against large concentrations of panzers, as they succumbed to large formations of Luftwaffe fighters and concentrated flak. Once again, their fighter escorts did not always demonstrate tactical acumen either. As before, the Yak-1s were often over-eager to engage in dogfights with their *Jagdwaffe* counterparts, exposing their charges to attack. As a result, there were heavy losses among the Il-2 units, while Soviet ground troops did not get the close air support they needed.

The losses of aircraft suffered by 9th SAK (*Smeshannyy Aviatsionnyy Korpus* – Composite Air Corps), 17th Air Army, which was primarily employed in attacking bridges over the Severskiy Donets River on 5-7 July, amounted to 55 per cent of its initial strength. Within the corps, 672nd ShAP lost 23 Il-2s, 995th ShAP 18, 991st ShAP 14, 237th ShAP 18, 175th ShAP 13 and 955th ShAP 17. The rate of loss was stunning, with one Il-2 being downed for every 2.8 sorties flown. Yet successes were achieved. The Germans' first attempt to cross the Severskiy Donets was repulsed during the night of 6 July, when six Il-2s from 955th ShAP, led by regimental CO Lt Col Bulanov, inflicted heavy losses on the enemy.

When General Staff officers examined the reasons for 9th SAK's losses, they noted that;

'Enemy air defence artillery around the targets was not suppressed. Only single aircraft were detailed to follow the group, which was not sufficient. About three to four groups would approach a target simultaneously and crowd around. Flight crews would not rendezvous as specified, and in other cases, unit commanders and group leaders failed to specify the rendezvous point and procedure clearly. Some pilots did not know the locations of operational airfields and runways on the way to and from the target, while COs did not brief their subordinates on emergency landing fields on the route back from the target.

'The escort fighters did not discharge their tasks to the full extent either between 5-8 July. While providing good protection on the way to the target, they climbed to a high altitude over the target, and thus lost sight of the Il-2 groups. After their target runs, attack aircraft would be engaged by enemy fighters and not receive the support of friendly fighters.'

BRIDGE-BUSTING

Within 5th GShAD and 290th ShAD of the 17th Air Army were two flights of Il-2s manned by crews who were specially trained to attack bridges – Red Army combat engineers had thrown pontoon bridges over the Severniy Donets to enable crews to practise such attacks. These two air divisions also had the greatest combat capability of any Il-2 units in the region, as more than half of their pilots had considerable frontline experience. Yet after the strike on Kramatorskaya airfield on the morning of 5 July, 5th GShAD was inexplicably held in reserve for the next three days. At the same time, the damage inflicted on the enemy by 290th ShAD had been considerably greater than that achieved by 9th SAK, and with significantly fewer losses in aircraft and aircrew.

Eight Il-2s from 625th ShAP, 290th ShAD, led by Capt Zakharov, achieved considerable success on 5 July when they attacked a German river crossing near Maslova Pristan. The Soviet aircraft approached the target in two columns at an altitude of 950 m (3000 ft), and as soon as the anti-aircraft guns opened up, the first group of four Il-2s pounced on them. The intensity of the flak was immediately reduced. The second group, led by Jnr Lt Miloshenkov, simultaneously bombed the bridge and strafed nearby vehicles and armour. After further attack runs, both groups descended to low level and raced back to Soviet-held territory without suffering any loss. The German river crossing had been wrecked.

All told, the pilots of 290th ShAD destroyed four river crossings and up to 40 vehicles during the course of the day. At the time, they could not put a figure on the extent of the destruction they had wrought due, they reported, to 'thick smoke, caused by numerous fires in the target area'.

The following day, 290th ShAD Il-2s destroyed two more bridges, four tanks, 41 vehicles, an anti-aircraft battery and a fuel depot. The regiment also destroyed five fighters at Tolokonnoe airfield and damaged ten more, and accounted for three Bf 109s and five Ju 52/3ms at Dudovka airfield. The *Shturmovik* pilots also engaged Luftwaffe aircraft over these bases, and during a series of five dogfights, the Il-2s claimed to have downed five Bf 109s, three Fw 190s, an Fw 189 and two Ju 88s towing gliders.

Maj Stolyarov of 775th ShAP, 290th ShAD deserves special mention for his initiative on this day. While leading six Il-2s to their assigned target, Stolyarov had spotted a concentration of enemy vehicles on the Kharkov-Belgorod road, two kilometres (1.25 miles) south of Tolokonnoe. As he neared the latter base in pursuit of the vehicles, he saw 50 Bf 109s and Fw 190s parked along the runway – it was possible that they had just landed and the groundcrews had not yet had the time to disperse them. Seizing his chance, Stolyarov decided to attack. Zooming up from low level to 300 m (1000 ft), the Il-2s dropped their bombs on the parked aircraft. Despite heavy flak, they did not suffer any loss. The crews' claims were confirmed by the escorting 207th IAD fighter pilots.

Stolyarov also distinguished himself on 7 July, when he led six Il-2s from 775th ShAP to attack a German convoy between Kharkov and Belgorod. Suddenly finding themselves over an airfield, the Soviet pilots spotted around 70 Luftwaffe aircraft. Stolyarov immediately ordered the element leaders to attack, and in the next few minutes 11 aircraft were destroyed on the ground, along with three Fw 190s caught attempting to take-off. The air gunners claimed to have shot shown three more Focke-Wulf fighters when they were set upon while leaving the target area.

As a result of these highly successful operations by 5th GShAD and 290th ShAD, VVS RKKA command and air army commanders

introduced numerous tactical changes in the Kursk salient. The days of independent flights of six/eight Il-2s, escorted by a few fighters, being sent to attack a series of targets over several hours would soon be gone. Close air support was now seen as a priority mission consisting of concentrated air strikes delivered by bombers and attack aircraft in regiment strength, escorted by a large number of fighters, together with in-depth operations by small groups of Il-2s sent to suppress flak defences.

From now on, the HQs of 15th and 1st Air Armies would plan all operations in strict coordination with the forces they were supporting on the ground. Each air army operated along the main axis of advance of the front to provide close air support to troops fighting within an area 10-12 km (6-7.5 miles) wide and 5-6 km (3-4 miles) deep during the breakthrough. At the same time, Il-2 crews focused their efforts on targets that might impede the advance, rather than spreading themselves widely.

Yet the air armies still failed to ensure this closely focused support was maintained throughout the offensive, coordinating their activities with ground troops on a tactical rather than operational level, and thus failing to provide on-the-spot support to the vulnerable armoured units in the vanguard of the advance. This in turn left the enemy free to summon up reserves located some 50-75 km (30-47 miles) away in rear areas.

The issue of efficient command and control over the battlefield remained to be solved, as Il-2s were often not guided directly by troops coming under enemy fire because of a paucity of command and control (C2) positions. Even when such control existed, cooperation between *Shturmoviks* and spotters was often poor. Air group COs would not always bother to establish communication with spotters, nor ask for frontline and target designation – sorties were often mounted at group leaders' discretion, rather in response to the situation on the ground.

Designation of friendly troops was also poor thanks to a shortage of signal panels and flares, especially after a few days of hostilities. Friendly troops were attacked in error on several occasions as a result.

A group of Il-2s have their engines run up prior to flying yet another combat sortie in the Kursk sector in the summer of 1943

There was a glaring example of such failures on 12 July, when Il-2s bombed and strafed Soviet ground forces at least five times during a counterattack near Prokhorovka, on the Voronezh Front. On the receiving end of these misdirected strikes were 32nd and 170th Tank Brigades, 92nd and 95th Guards Rifle Divisions and 4th Guards Motorised Rifle Brigade. That same day, 13 Il-2s from 233rd ShAD, 1st Air Army, supporting the Western Front offensive, made two attack runs on friendly troops near Ozhigovo. *Shturmoviks* from 15th Air Army, operating in the Bryansk Front's offensive area, did the same at least eight times that month, while the Central Front sustained 11 such strikes by 16th Air Army aircraft between 9 July and 9 August.

Yet there are many archive documents which demonstrate that where Il-2s acted correctly, great success was achieved and ground troops were able to advance rapidly. On 7 July, 7th Guards Army commander Gen Shumilov was able to praise 290th ShAD crews for their performance when they attacked German tanks and mechanised infantry near Yastrebovo and Bessonovka. Similarly, the chief-of-staff of 24th Rifle Corps expressed his gratitude to pilots for a strike by eight Il-2s near Maslova Pristan that same day. On 8 July, Shumilov again praised 290th ShAD crews for two attacks near Razumnoe which inflicted such losses on a German tank convoy that it was forced to turn back.

On the 9th, 17th Air Army Il-2s dispersed a convoy of panzers and mechanised infantry near Maslova Pristan. The tanks were being refuelled when the Il-2s made their first run-in, and three concentrated passes drove the enemy to seek cover in a forest west of the Polyana collective farm on the southern edge of the Dacha Shebeninskaya estate.

This particular attack on *Wehrmacht* tanks was one of the first to be made by Il-2s armed with 37 mm NS-37 cannon and PTAB-2.5-1.5 shaped-charge anti-tank bombs – both weapons would play their part in securing Soviet success in the Battle of Kursk. The NS-37 armour-piercing round enabled Soviet pilots to knock out light and medium tanks, including the much-vaunted PzKpfw V Panther, while the PTAB could destroy any *Wehrmacht* tank. Capable of penetrating up to 60 mm of armour, the small bomb was carried in clusters of 280 by the Il-2. This ensured a high probability of hits against enemy tanks even when they were in open formations. The footprint of bombs dropped by a single aircraft could cover two to three tanks spaced 60-75 m (200-250 ft) apart.

But despite the urgency, not enough Il-2 tank-busters were being built, and nor was there sufficient conversion training for crews assigned to fly them. Although no NS-37-armed Il-2s had been delivered when the Battle of Kursk started, many PTAB-2.5-1.5 bombs had indeed reached frontline units.

These weapons were used in combat for the first time on the morning of 5 July 1943 on the Voronezh Front when eight crews from 617th ShAP, 291st ShAD, 2nd Air Army attacked tanks of the German 48th Panzer Corps as they headed for Cherkasskoe. The Il-2s hit another concentration of tanks two kilometres north of Butovo, with pilots reporting seeing explosions, fire and thick smoke following their attacks – up to 15 tanks and six vehicles were destroyed. During this attack, the Soviet crews expended 1248 PTAB bombs, eight AO-25 fragmentation bombs, 28 RS-82 rockets and 890 VYa-23 cannon rounds.

Pilots from 266th ShAD, 1st ShAK also used PTAB bombs that day when a group of ten Il-2s from 673rd ShAP, led by regimental CO Maj Matikov, attacked stationary tanks near Yakovlevo and Pogorelovo. Up to ten panzers and ten vehicles were destroyed or damaged by the 491 PTABs, high-explosive and fragmentation bombs that were dropped.

The PTAB had indeed made an impressive combat debut. In his report to Air Force Commander Marshal Novikov, Gen Khudyakov stated that 'Col Vitruk's pilots marvel at the effect of these bombs'. As a result, the Soviet command chose to employ the PTAB on a large scale in attacks on the Central and the Voronezh Fronts the very next day (6th).

Attack aircraft from 2nd Air Army dropped 11,703 PTABs on enemy tanks, while 16th Air Army used 1784. The scale of the PTABs' employment increased still further on the 7th, when 2nd Air Army dropped 14,272 and 16th Air Army 7585. The leading tank-busting units were 299th and 291st ShADs, with their regiments dropping the lion's share of the PTABs. On 9 July, 17th Air Army started using them too, and three days later, during the Orel offensive, aircraft from the 1st and 15th Air Armies of the Western and Bryansk Fronts followed suit.

This massive employment of PTABs not only created surprise on a tactical scale but also significantly undermined enemy morale. German tank crews, just like their Soviet counterparts, had become used to relatively ineffective air strikes over the previous two years. Panzer units were to pay dearly for their delay in adopting more open formations. The former chief-of-staff of the German 48th Panzer Corps, Gen von Mellenthin, wrote later that 'many tanks fell prey to the Soviet aircraft, despite the German air superiority, and the Russian pilots displayed exceptional valour during this battle'.

Flight crews reported that direct PTAB hits set enemy tanks and vehicles alight, and also that the Germans would leave the road and disperse for fear of follow-up air strikes. The claims by pilots using the bombs were so extensive that they were often doubted by superior officers. Engineer Maj Pimenov, a senior assistant chief of the 2nd Department of the Air Force General Staff Operations Directorate, explained why in a report he wrote after a tour with 16th Air Army;

'Flight personnel debriefings cannot be objective since attack aircraft pilots do not see their bombs hit the targets. They can only claim kills by indirect signs, therefore. These may be billowing smoke in the overall cloud of dust or powerful explosions, which could be caused by their own heavy bombs, especially as aircraft in a group usually carry a mixed assortment of bomb loads.'

In light of such scepticism, divisional staff officers and regimental commanders started flying combat missions to monitor the results of air strikes in person. Air armies' headquarters also assigned special groups to their subordinate units to test the claims. On 7 July, Military Engineer Second Rank Shcherbina, deputy commander of 299th ShAD for air gunnery, accompanied a group of seven 217th ShAP Il-2s led by Snr Lt Ryzhkov. His mission was to assess the results of a strike on panzers deployed on a hill one kilometre north of Ponyri railway station. Reconnaissance flights had detected up to 50 tanks, about 35 of which had been dug in. Two Il-2s carried PTABs while the rest were armed with FAB-50s.

Diving on the panzers at an angle of 20-25 degrees from an altitude of 800-900 m (2600-3000 ft), the *Shturmoviks* made two passes over the target area. PTABs hit the tanks and set three on fire, with flames and black smoke billowing from them.

On 8 July, 617th ShAP CO, Maj Lomovtsev, headed a group of six Il-2s whose target was enemy tanks near Pokrovka, Yakovlevo and Kozmo-Demyanovka. The crews made two attack runs, dropping PTAB bombs from 600-800 m (2000-2600 ft) on the first and strafing the tanks from 150-200 m (500-650 ft) on the second. As they left the target, crews noted four powerful explosions and up to 15 burning tanks.

The result of such sorties in which senior commanders and staff officers could see the extent of the damage with their own eyes enabled the air armies' commands to state that 'the enemy losses statistics cited were correct', and that they could be trusted. Such a report was issued by the VVS RKKA General Staff Operations Directorate on 12 July;

'The encrypted message sent by Col Gen Vorozheykin to Stalin on 11 July 1943 says that Soviet ground troops deployed on Hill 255.1 (the Central Front) saw six Il-2s attack 15 Tiger tanks, setting six of them on fire. A large panzer force was detected on a hill east of Kashary (the Central Front) on 10 July. Soviet attack aircraft delivered a pin-point air strike, killing 30 enemy tanks and setting 14 on fire, while the rest of the panzer group dispersed and started a chaotic retreat northwards.'

According to archive documents, 2nd Tank Army and 13th Army headquarters reported that massive air strikes north of Ponyri, Pervye Ponyri, and Hill 238.1, as well as Kashary, Severnye Kutyrki and Hill 257.0, on 10 July resulted in the destruction of up to 48 German tanks. They also state that the enemy was forced to halt its attacks and withdraw its remaining forces to an area north of Kashary. 16th Air Army headquarters, reported that 39 tanks were destroyed by Il-2s from 2nd GShAD and 299th ShAD, with five more being credited to 3rd BAK (*Bombardirovochnyy Aviatsionyy Korpus* – Bomber Aviation Corps) crews. The *Shturmoviks* were armed exclusively with PTAB bombs.

PTAB DESTRUCTION

The devastating effect a PTAB had on a tank was quickly revealed to Soviet forces in the wake of these missions in early July when a special commission inspected two target areas in which the weapon had been recently used. It found six panzers

Capt V B Emelyanenko of 7th GShAP smiles for the camera in the cockpit of his aircraft at an airfield near the village of Timoshevskaya, near Krasnodar, in August 1943. A member of the composer department of the Moscow Conservatory pre-war, Emelyanenko arrived at his unit with a balalaika! Note that his aircraft was also adorned with a musical emblem on its fuselage, applied by regimental artist Aleksandr Bulyndenko. The Il-2 also featured a Guards emblem immediately behind the cockpit

Maj Lomovtsev, 617th ShAP CO, commends squadron leader Sen Lt Garin on a successful combat mission in the Belgorod sector in August 1943

This photo of 59th GShAP squadron leader Capt A A Bondar was taken on 1 October 1943 on the Central Front. Bondar was killed in action four weeks later on 28 October. According to official sources, he destroyed 70 panzers and eight German aircraft. Bondar was posthumously awarded the title of HSU

Also photographed on 1 October 1943 on the Central Front was 59th GShAP squadron leader Capt A I Kadomtsev. Official sources state that he destroyed 60 panzers and 20 aircraft. He died when he dived his burning Il-2 into a concentration of German military equipment on 21 February 1944. Capt Kadomtsev was also posthumously awarded the title of HSU on 13 April 1944

and 16 self-propelled guns destroyed, four of which had been by struck by PTABs. Examination showed that in most cases a tank could not be repaired after a PTAB hit. The commission stated;

'Fire caused by a PTAB hit destroys every piece of equipment, the tank armour becomes annealed and loses its protective qualities and a detonation of the ammunition stowage finishes the tank off.'

One of the tanks examined was a German Ferdinand 88 mm tank-hunter destroyed by a PTAB five kilometres (three miles) northeast of Ponyri railway station. The bomb had hit the armour plate over the vehicle's portside fuel tank, penetrated 20 mm of armour, burst the fuel tank and ignited the petrol. Fire had destroyed every piece of hardware within the hull itself, detonated the ammunition stowage and destroyed the breech of the gun, which still had a round inside it. The floor had collapsed and the armour was covered with a pink deposit, signifying that it had lost its physicochemical properties. The commission concluded, 'The self-propelled gun is an irreplaceable loss since it is impossible to repair it'. Two more burnt out Ferdinands were found 1.5 km east of Buzuluki and 1.5 km north of Ponyri railway station.

An assault gun based on the PzKpfw IV tank chassis was also discovered near Ponyri. It had been destroyed when its ammunition store blew up. PTAB craters were spotted around the wrecked self-propelled guns.

The commission thought that as most of these armoured vehicles were attacked in staging areas and refuelling depots, or while coming from rear areas, the Germans might be able to recover some of them. It therefore concluded that 'in fact, the number of enemy tanks and self-propelled guns destroyed by PTABs may be considerably higher'.

Further confirmation of the PTAB's effectiveness came from an unexpected source. A Soviet tank company, advancing in the offensive sector controlled by 380th Rifle Division of the Bryansk Front near the village of Podmaslovo, was mistakenly attacked by Il-2s. One T-34 suffered a direct hit from a PTAB and duly broke into several parts. A commission of investigation later reported that it had found 'seven craters around the tank, as well as burning PTAB-2.5-1.5 fragments'. Archive documents also show that Soviet attack aircraft hit two PzKpfw VI Tiger main battle tanks in the same area as well.

The attacking aircraft were probably a group of four Il-2s from 614th ShAP, 225th ShAD, headed by Capt Chubuk. They attacked up to 25 German tanks, including ten Tigers, making a counterattack on 15 July. The Soviet pilots dropped a total of 1190 PTAB bombs while flying level at 130-150 m (400-500 ft), and they reported destroying seven tanks, including four heavy ones.

The victory claims, and general praise for the PTAB expressed by the attack units, enabled Engineer Maj Pimenov to report to his superiors that 'PTAB air bombs solved the major problem of the low efficiency of air strikes on enemy armour, which is inherent in high-explosive and fragmentation bombs – namely a low hit probability because of the ratio of the target area to the bomb footprint on the ground'.

Gen Zhuravlev, Chief of the VVS RKKA General Staff Operations Directorate, was able to conclude that the weapons 'should be launched into mass production and be employed on a large scale in air strikes on enemy mechanised forces, trains, river crossings, weapon emplacements

59th GShAP Il-2 of Lt V F Ignatiev is prepared for a combat sortie by aircraft armament technician Gunnery Lance Corporal N N Okuneva (left) and aircraft technician Sgt L S Shnaydruk on the Central Front on 1 October 1943. Okuneva appears to checking one of the VYa 23 mm cannon magazines prior to fitting it back into the wing

Having finished checking the magazines, Gunnery Lance Corporal N N Okuneva now sets about preparing rocket projectiles for Lt V F Ignatiev's Il-2

and similar targets. PTABs successfully destroy such targets'.

Recovering from the initial shock of the PTAB, German tank units soon adopted open formations. Such tactics in turn adversely affected command and control efficiency, speed of deployment, concentration and interoperability, but resulted in a sharp decline in the effectiveness of strikes by Il-2s using PTABs. Even with these revised tactics, the kill rate for the *Shturmoviks* with the new weapon was still considerably better than that previously achieved with conventional high-explosive and fragmentation bombs.

AZh-2 incendiary bombs also became popular with Il-2 units at this time due to their effectiveness against both armour and anti-aircraft batteries. This was demonstrated to Military Engineer Second Rank Shcherbina from 299th ShAD headquarters, who was able to report to his superiors that 'excellent results' had been achieved by eight 218th ShAP Il-2s, led by Snr Lt Slavitskiy, when they attacked enemy vehicles, tanks and light anti-aircraft guns near Rzhavets.

Shcherbina recounted that when two Il-2s dropped AZh-2 clusters on the artillery positions, 'I saw several dozen bright-red explosions, and 20 seconds later the target area was covered with thick white smoke. Incendiary bottles, dropped on air defence artillery batteries, killed gun crews and, as a result, enemy flak near Rzhavets decreased considerably'.

Il-2 tank-busters armed with NS-37 cannon did not appear in sizeable numbers at the front until August, when they were deployed by 568th ShAP (231st ShAD) and 801st ShAP (32nd ShAD) of 2nd ShAK, operating as part of 1st Air Army on the Western Front. The following month, the new aircraft entered service with 1st ShAK, and in October-November it entered the inventory of 7th ShAK, 1st GShAD and 227th ShAD. Pilots noted that the new Il-2 was less manoeuvrable and controllable than the non-cannon *Shturmovik*, and when the two NS-37 weapons were fired, they caused the aircraft to pitch and yaw violently. Each burst was therefore limited to three or four rounds.

Despite these problems, the NS-37 proved to be a formidable weapon. Indeed, pilots of 568th ShAP used their cannon-equipped Il-2s to destroy six tanks and self-propelled guns, 99 motor vehicles, ten wagons and six artillery pieces between 15 and 26 September.

According to 1st ShAK documents, pilots had discovered several ways of destroying targets with the

NS-37. On 6 October, Jnr Lt Samorodov fired a short burst in an effort to break the track of a German tank, which turned around and stopped. Three days later, Lt Voskonin set two enemy tanks on fire with short and accurate bursts from a range of 250-300m (275-330 yards).

Yet despite the high efficiency shown by pilots flying NS-37-equipped Il-2s, flight personnel and commanding officers of 1st and 2nd ShAK thought that the new attack aircraft was not better than the VYa-23 23 mm cannon-armed Il-2. In their view, 'the VYa cannon, ensuring a high density of fire on the ground, was the most efficient armament mounted on the Il-2.' They also added that a combination of the VYa cannon and PTAB air bombs provided for a higher kill probability.

In practice, NS-37-armed Il-2s could only be successfully employed if the battlefield environment allowed them to make several runs on the target, as they could fire only a few rounds at a time. They also carried a much smaller bomb load than VYa-equipped aircraft. 'Thus, they could not ensure reliable destruction of the target', the reported concluded.

The State Defence Committee ordered series production of Il-2s armed with NS-37s to be terminated on 12 November. Presumably, the results achieved by 37 mm cannon-armed Il-2s were not as impressive as those of aircraft using PTABs. Documents state that most pilots would be unable to kill tanks using NS-37s installed in Il-2s in a combat environment. At the same time, it would take too long to train selected pilots in the weapon's use – PTAB employment did not require special training.

ON THE OFFENSIVE

When the Voronezh and the Stepnoy Fronts launched an advance on Belgorod-Kharkov on 3 August, the German command immediately started redeploying its reserves to the 4th Panzer Army. Soviet aerial reconnaissance reported enemy tank and motorised convoys moving north on the very first day of the offensive. Twenty-four hours later, VVS RKKA commenced operations to disrupt enemy supply routes, with the main burden associated with these missions being shouldered by 17th Air Army. It was ordered to attack road and rail traffic in the Kramatorskaya, Lozovaya, Kharkov and Belgorod areas.

Although 290th ShAD, 3rd SAK was the only Il-2 unit properly equipped to carry out this mission within the first three days of the offensive being launched, the results it achieved were considered significant nevertheless. On 4 August, two groups of six Il-2s each, escorted by fighters from 207th IAD, attacked trains carrying tanks, motor vehicles and troops at both Gusarovka railway station and Troychatiy junction at 1423-1524 hrs and 1645-1802 hrs, respectively. They destroyed two locomotives, 30 goods wagons and platform trucks, together with 16 vehicles and an ammunition dump at Gusarovka.

The following day, six groups of six Il-2s each attacked forces moving from Kharkov to Belgorod, as well as troop trains in the Krasnopavlovka and Likhachevo areas, and at Troychatiy junction. The crews claimed to have completely destroyed five troop trains, each made up of 30-40 goods wagons, as well as an additional two locomotives and up to 32 goods wagons and platform trucks. Their claims were confirmed by the escorting fighter pilots and by the crew of a reconnaissance aircraft, which had been detailed to monitor the target area.

Pilots of 7th GShAP discuss their latest combat mission as they walk away from their Il-2s in August 1943. Nikolay Ostapenko (third left) destroyed his target on his first attack run, and he is illustrating just how he did this to his fellow pilots. The musically-inclined Capt V B Emelyanenko is at first left

Six Il-2s from 775th ShAP, headed by Jnr Lt Sibirkin, were particularly successful on 6 August when they attacked a troop train on the Tarakanovka-Troychatiy line. The Il-2s damaged the engine, blew up four tanker trucks loaded with fuel and destroyed a platform truck carrying vehicles. And that was just on their first attacking pass! Other rolling stock subsequently caught fire and the entire train was eventually burnt out.

Crews from 290th ShAD flew 88 combat sorties the next day, destroying three troop trains, a locomotive, five tanker trucks, 12 goods wagons and about 125 vehicles. Jnr Lt Maslennikov of 775th ShAP demonstrated outstanding valour during one of these missions. The Il-2 piloted by group leader Maj Stolyarov was hit by flak during an attack on a convoy of tanks and mechanised infantry on the Mechebilovka-Gorokhovka road, and the pilot crash-landed two kilometres away. Maslennikov immediately landed nearby to pick him up. His Il-2 was a single-seat aircraft, however, so the lieutenant gave up his seat to the more experienced Stolyarov and, together with the air gunner, clambered inside the fuselage of the *Shturmovik*.

While all this was going on, the other pair of Il-2s covered their comrades by machine gunning German soldiers to keep them away from the landing site. Shortly after take-off, the engine of the heavily-laden aircraft started overheating, so as soon as they crossed Severskiy Donets, Stolyarov landed at Levkovka airfield. Maslennikov received the Order of the Red Banner and was promoted to senior lieutenant for his brave deed.

Ground attack support for operations by the Voronezh and the Stepnoy Fronts near the end of the Battle of Kursk ultimately involved 51 Il-2 groups and 104 fighter groups from 17th Air Army. *Shturmovik* units flew a total of 966 combat sorties, during which they destroyed ten locomotives, 170 goods wagons and 526 vehicles, plus six ammunition dumps and fuel depots.

The Red Army's successful operations during the Battles of Kursk and Orel created the conditions for an all-out offensive to liberate Eastern Ukraine, cross the Dnieper River and secure footholds on its right bank.

The aftermath of yet another Il-2 air strike! A German motor convoy lies shattered where it was attacked during the Battle of Kursk

To commemorate the victory over the *Wehrmacht*, the People's Commissar of Defence issued an order on 24 August 1943 converting 3rd SAK into 1st GSAK. Both 207th IAD and 290th ShAD also received Guards titles, becoming 11th GIAD and 6th GShAD, respectively. 232nd ShAD, 2nd ShAK, was transformed into 7th GShAK on 3 September 1943.

THE FINAL STAGES

Following victories in the Battles of Kursk and Orel, the liberation of western Ukraine and the Crimea were the objectives set by the Supreme High Command General Headquarters for the Red Army in its next major campaign in the Great Patriotic War. Once again, the Il-2 would in the vanguard of the action.

Between late December 1943 and mid-April 1944, one of the war's largest battles unfolded from Polesye to the Black Sea and from the Dnieper River to the Carpathian Mountains. The four Ukrainian Fronts were set the task of destroying the *Wehrmacht's* Army Group South and Army Group A. On 29 December, Soviet high command decided to launch a large-scale offensive aimed at encircling and destroying enemy forces at Kirovograd. This campaign was to commence no later than 5 January. The main attack was directed at Kirovograd and Pervomaysk, with secondary advances on Shpola and Khristinovka. Ground troops were to be supported by 5th Air Army.

Operations on the first day of the campaign were hampered by low cloud and thick fog, and, as a result, 734 combat sorties were flown instead of the planned 1120. The weather improved the following day, and Soviet pilots were able to deliver several powerful blows against German strongpoints and pockets of resistance, as well as the roads and rail lines to Kirovograd. Crews from 1st ShAK were especially successful.

Capt Poshivalnikov led 12 Il-2s from 800th ShAP, 292nd ShAD, to strike tanks and artillery southwest of Adzhamki – they destroyed a total of five enemy vehicles. While recovering from his third run over the target, Poshivalnikov noticed four Bf 109s closing in. He immediately ordered his group to form a defensive circle, and one of the Messerschmitts was shot down in the ensuing dogfight.

Another group of 18 Il-2s from 673rd ShAP, 266th ShAD, headed by Maj Matikov, also achieved success. Tanks, vehicles and troops were attacked near Zavadovka, and the crews claimed to have accounted for seven vehicles and about 100 troops. Twelve 800th ShAP Il-2 pilots led by Capt Stepanov were credited with the destruction of two tanks and three vehicles. They also reported causing two powerful explosions and suppressing two field artillery batteries on the southern edge of Marievka, near Oboznovka. Seven 66th ShAP, 266th ShAD Il-2s headed by Lt Pushkin accounted for six vehicles on the road between Bratolyubovka and Gurovka. They also blew up an ammunition dump.

But the fiercest battle of the day, which involved a large number of tanks, was fought near Novgorodka. Both sides used their air power on a large scale, with Il-2s from 1st ShAK attacking ground targets and engaging in dogfights. After attacking German tanks, four *Shturmoviks* from 735th ShAP, 266th ShAD encountered three groups of Ju 87s that were slightly above them and preparing to strike Soviet troops. The Il-2 group leader, Lt Filatov, decided to attack the dive-bombers, and two of the Stukas were quickly shot down – one was claimed by Filatov. The

Serious-looking air- and groundcrew gunners from 6th GShAP receive a mission briefing in the Baltic in March 1945

Commander of 1st GShAK, twice HSU Lt Gen of Aviation V G Ryazanov

remaining Stukas hastily dropped their bombs and headed home.

Elsewhere on 6 January, nine 66th ShAP Il-2s, led by Capt Devyatyarov, engaged in a fierce air battle with eight Bf 109s. The German pilots had attacked the Soviet aircraft as they completed their first passes on a column of tanks. Four Bf 109s kept the escorting fighters occupied, while the other four attacked the Il-2s head-on. For once the Luftwaffe pilots were out of luck, however, and air gunners Sgt Manashkin and Pte Barannikov succeeded in shooting down three Messerschmitts between them.

These successful clashes reveal just how much the Soviet attack aircraft pilots had improved their tactical competence and combat skills during two-and-a-half years of near-constant fighting. They were now operating in strict compliance with the prevailing environment during each combat sortie, and thus inflicting significant manpower and equipment losses on the enemy. They were also able to minimise their own losses, as the dogfights on 6 January showed. That day, 1st ShAK flight crews had flown a total of 348 combat sorties and destroyed 26 tanks, 112 vehicles and seven field and air defence artillery batteries. They were also credited with downing seven enemy aircraft. Only two Il-2s were lost in return.

This increase in effective aerial activity had an immediate impact on the combat environment, and helped facilitate a Soviet breakthrough of the German defences. Up to 15,000 enemy troops had been encircled in the Lepekovka and Balka-Zlodeyka areas by the end of 6 January, and a series of counterattacks were mounted by the *Wehrmacht* in an effort to rescue them. These involved a large number of tanks and mechanised troops.

Soviet air reconnaissance detected two large convoys of German tanks and vehicles moving out of Novonikolaevka and Pyatikhatki towards Oboznovka on 7 January, and attack aircraft from 1st ShAK were scrambled to destroy them. The first group of seven Il-2s was headed by 667th ShAP squadron leader Capt Kompaniets, who was one of 292nd ShAD's most experienced pilots. Despite thick fog, the crews spotted the enemy on the south-western outskirts of Lepekovka and destroyed five tanks, ten vehicles and two infantry companies in several attack passes.

The second group of seven Il-2s, led by Capt Krasota (a squadron leader from the 667th ShAP), appeared immediately afterwards, and in a 20-minute attack, they accounted for 16 troop-laden trucks. Such strikes helped 29th Tank Corps repulse the enemy counterattacks and then go on the offensive and liberate several populated areas.

The following day saw a continuation of 1st ShAK's strikes on the encircled *Wehrmacht* troops. Given the complex combat environment on the ground, 1st ShAK commander Lt Gen V G Ryazanov personally guided the attack aircraft from the 5th Guards Army command post. Despite adverse weather and the proximity of the targets to the frontline, corps pilots demonstrated their high level of competency. No attacks on

69

friendly troops were reported throughout the day, while heavy losses in manpower and equipment were inflicted on the enemy.

A group of nine 673rd ShAP Il-2s headed by Sen Lt Aleksandrov attacked a motorised convoy two kilometres (1.25 miles) southwest of Lepekovka and destroyed ten vehicles. Another group of eight Il-2s from 800th ShAP, led by Capt Poshivalnikov, left ten vehicles and a fuel tanker burning in ravines southwest of Lepekovka. Finally, Capt Lopatin led nine Il-2s from 667th ShAP in the destruction of 18 vehicles and mortar batteries in six attack runs in the same area.

By 10 January the encircled German forces had been defeated. Lt Gen Ryazanov personally inspected the battlefield, and determined that corps attack aircraft had destroyed or damaged about 400 vehicles, 52 tanks and 50 self-propelled guns in the Lepekovka and Balka Zlodeyka areas. Enemy supply routes were also disrupted.

That same day, when reconnaissance aircraft detected enemy trains carrying combat vehicles at Smela station, Ryazanov called for volunteers from among the most experienced pilots in his command to attack, despite thick fog and pouring rain. The mission was assigned to Lts Mikhaylichenko and Chechelashvili from 667th ShAP.

To ensure surprise, the pair plotted a course that would see them flying mostly over heavily wooded (and sparsely populated) areas that were in German hands as they approached the target. Flying at low level deep into enemy territory, Mikhaylichenko eventually sighted steam some three kilometres (two miles) from the station. The pilots zoomed up as high as the cloud cover would allow and then commenced a gentle glide in the direction of the target. Initially launching their rocket projectiles, they then strafed and bombed the trains. By the time Mikhaylichenko and his wingman left, the station was ablaze and ammunition was exploding.

The surprise the pilots had achieved was shown in the fact that there had initially been no anti-aircraft fire opposing them on their first pass. However, as they approached on their second attack run, German gunners opened up with a heavy flak barrage that stretched from the edge of the forest all the way to the station. Mikhaylichenko's aircraft was damaged and he was forced to turn back. His engine stopped just short of the River Dnieper, and he hastily crash-landed in no-man's land. The Germans immediately attacked the Il-2 with mortar fire, but Mikhaylichenko and his air gunner managed to reach Soviet positions.

The Second Ukrainian Front launched an offensive near Novoukrainka on 15 January. At 0850 hrs, 1st ShAK Il-2s laid smoke screens to conceal the advancing infantry and tanks. Ten minutes later, six groups of nine Pe-2s from 1st BAK bombed German forces near Bolshaya Viska, Blagodatnoe and Novoaleksandrovka. Between 0950 hrs and 1040 hrs, four groups of nine Il-2s struck strong points at Andreevka, Aleksandrovka and Ovsyanikova and two groups of nine Petlyakov Pe-2s bombed enemy positions near Maryanovka and Fedorovka.

While the Soviet aircraft went into action above them, artillery gunners laid down a creeping barrage that allowed infantry units and tanks to advance, supported by the Il-2s of 1st ShAK. Throughout the day *Shturmoviks* cleared the way for advancing Soviet troops.

At noon, seven 800th ShAP Il-2s, led by Capt Poshivalnikov, attacked a strongpoint on the eastern outskirts of Aleksandrovka. The Soviet pilots

The squadron personnel of 15th GShAP are, standing (from left to right), Temchuk, Valentin Averyanov, Nikolay Polagushini, Medvedev, Shulzhenko, and seated (from left to right), Sergey Potapov, Aleksandr Manokhin and Evgeniy Kungurtsev

made three runs over the target, setting several vehicles alight and wiping out two platoons of infantry. Elsewhere, eight 667th ShAP Il-2s, headed by Sen Lt Lopatin, attacked a *Wehrmacht* stronghold near Novoaleksandrovka. Soviet troops confirmed that the 15-minute attack launched at 1315 hrs had resulted in the destruction of three vehicles, a tank and a field artillery battery. The group then fought off four Bf 109s, downing one without suffering any losses in return.

Even though the Soviet forces captured the Blagodatnoe-Ivanovka area on the first day of the offensive, the advance stalled in the face of non-stop German counterattacks. Then, on the 18th, the weather deteriorated when a sharp rise in the temperature brought the cloud base down to 100-300 m (300-1000 ft) and reduced visibility to 500 m (1600 ft) or less. The area was also blighted with constant rain and fog. Most aircraft were confined to their airfields, and 5th Air Army could only send its most skilful crews aloft. These few Il-2s free-hunted singly or in pairs over the battlefield and in rear areas immediately behind the frontline.

By 19 January it had become clear that 5th Guards Tank Army was exhausted and could no longer advance. It had to be withdrawn, and there were not sufficient Soviet reserves available to complete the encirclement of the German Eighth Field Army in the Kanev salient and advance further west. Despite falling short of its ultimate objective, the Kirovograd operation had enabled Soviet forces to inflict significant losses on the enemy, and advance westwards by up to 50 km (31 miles).

The Il-2 crews' achievements during the Kursk operation in the summer of 1943, and in the recent offensive in western Ukraine, were officially recognised on 5 February 1944 when 1st ShAK became 1st GShAK and 291st ShAD was redesignated 10th GShAD. Divisions of the former 1st ShAK were simultaneously transformed into Guards divisions, with 266th ShAD becoming 8th GShAD, 292nd ShAD redesignated as 9th GShAD and 203rd IAD changing to 12th GIAD.

MAJOR OFFENSIVE

Although the Germans had managed to halt the Soviet offensive at Novoukrainka and elsewhere, the Red Army began further advances in the Nikopolsko-Krivorozhskaya and Korsun-Shevchenkovskaya areas in March. These campaigns were not only victorious, but dealt a real knockout blow to Army Group South. The Soviet command followed this up in the summer with the brilliantly successful Byelorussian strategic offensive against Army Group Centre.

The command's objective was to simultaneously break through the enemy's defensive lines in six directions. First, frontal attacks were to be launched, then enemy forces near Vitebsk, Bobruysk, Minsk, Orsha and Mogilev were to be encircled and destroyed. The main Red Army air forces involved included 3rd, 1st, 4th and 16th Air Armies, while 6th Air

Army joined the battle during its second stage. All told, 15 attack aircraft divisions – including three Guards divisions (1st, 2nd and 3rd GShADs) and 6th Independent Guards Attack Aircraft Regiment – equipped with 2000+ Il-2s participated in the offensive.

The 1st Baltic Front and 2nd and 3rd Byelorussian Fronts mounted a general offensive on 23 June. The right wing of the 1st Byelorussian Front launched an offensive the following morning. Actively supported by attack aircraft, 65th and 28th Armies breached enemy defences south of Parichi and drove a 30-km (19-mile) wide wedge on the very first day of the offensive. Thrown into the gap, 1st Guards Tank Corps managed to fight its way 20 km (12.5 miles) into the enemy's rear. This unit was supported by 2nd GShAD, whose 40 Il-2s appeared over Soviet tanks at the appointed time, and 15 minutes later they were joined by an additional 35 *Shturmoviks*.

Providing close air support to ground troops in these circumstances was not an easy task for the attack aircraft pilots. Soviet tank spearheads frequently moved ahead of enemy rear units, and it was difficult for aircrews to decide which were friendly forces and which were hostile. Coordination between Il-2 units and troops on the ground was now much improved, and two groups of six aircraft from 2nd GShAD, led by Lts Gorbatenko and Gribov, proved this on the 24th.

Tasked with attacking enemy forces at Baraniy Rog, as the Il-2s approached the 1st Guards Tank Corps command post, they learned that the Soviet tank units' advance had been halted by heavy artillery fire. Gen Komarov, commander of 2nd GShAD, was at the command post, and he ordered Gribov to search for German artillery units dug in near the village of Chernye Borody and its local railway station. Gribov soon reported the presence of an artillery battalion on the village's south-western outskirts. In six attacking passes, the Il-2s silenced the artillery, thus enabling the tanks to capture Chernye Borody without suffering heavy losses.

On 26 June, 9th Tank Corps completed the northern striking force's breakthrough and had reached the River Berezina by day's end. The southern force bypassed Bobruysk from the southwest, leaving attack aircraft to destroy the retreating enemy convoys on the roads, demolish bridges over the Berezina and fly reconnaissance missions. Meanwhile, 4th ShAK, 2nd GShAD and 299th ShAD provided close air support to 9th and 1st Guards Tank Corps and 4th Guards Cavalry Corps. The Il-2s flew a total of 858 combat sorties during the course of the day.

In order to further enhance cooperation between air and ground units, air division commanding officers started basing themselves within the observation posts of the ground units that they were assigned to support. Spotters were

Soviet attack aircraft destroyed these German StuG 40 assault guns in the Riga sector in 1944

also attached to first-echelon units in the frontline so as to provide target designation information for flight crews.

On the 26th, one such spotter from 299th ShAD ordered Il-2 group leader Maj Seliverstov to 'attack enemy troops and vehicles north of Ozemlya and on the road west of the railway'. Identifying the spotter's divisional radio station by its codeword, Seliverstov and his group duly attacked the specified target. The station spotter confirmed the attack following each run, and after the fifth pass he radioed 'Nice work. Head for home. A second group is on the way'.

Corps political officer Col Karev noted in his report on the Il-2's combat operation;

'Aviation is operating well in providing close air support to the corps. Groups of attack aircraft and fighters succeeded each other non-stop throughout 26 June. They inflicted considerable losses on the enemy and defended the corps from the air. Our corps, which had fought on other fronts as well, had never seen such well coordinated aviation efforts.'

As previously mentioned in this chapter, on the third day of the offensive, the 1st Byelorussian Front bypassed enemy forces near Bobruysk to the north and cut off their withdrawal routes to the west. Retreating into the town itself, German combat vehicles and troop convoys were aggressively hunted down by Soviet attack aircraft. And for the latter, there was no shortage of targets. Indeed, one reconnaissance aircraft alone sighted a convoy comprising up to 600 vehicles in the 65th Army offensive sector. Some 44 Il-2s from 300th ShAD were quickly scrambled to destroy it, and small groups of Soviet attack aircraft kept the convoy under constant attack for almost two hours. As a result, the German retreat was halted and the vehicles dispersed, but not before more than 100 of them had been destroyed.

On the morning of 27 June, 4th ShAK Il-2s struck motorised convoys on the Bortnikov-Titovka, Titovka-Bobruysk and Bobruysk-Osipovichi roads. They destroyed up to 600 trucks and 40 tanks and armoured personnel carriers, and a large number of troops were also killed.

Later that same day, aerial reconnaissance reported that much of the German Ninth Field Army – six divisions – had been encircled southeast of Bobruysk. The enemy had concentrated a large number of tanks, field guns, trucks and infantry in the villages of Savichi, Telusha, Stupeni and Dubovka, as well as in nearby forests, in order to attempt a breakout after nightfall. With these targets having been spotted less than three hours prior to dusk, the Soviets needed to mount a rapid strike.

A total of 523 combat aircraft, including 175 bombers and 217 Il-2s, were scrambled by the 16th Air Army. Attack aircraft from 4th ShAK (196th and 199th ShADs), 2nd GShAD and 299th ShAD were ordered to destroy equipment and troop concentrations, and to do so without fighter escort. They were also ordered to bomb the tanks and strafe the troops, operating from 400-600 m (1250-2000 ft) down to very low level. Finally, the Il-2 crews were told to stay over these target areas for as long as possible, making several attack runs and suppressing defensive artillery whenever encountered.

The first groups of Soviet bombers appeared over the Bobruysk pocket at 1915 hrs. The encircled German forces opened up heavy anti-aircraft fire, but the Il-2s commenced flak suppression almost immediately. The

16th Air Army Il-2s were particularly severe on retreating German forces near Bobruysk on 27 June 1944. This was the aftermath of one such attack near the village of Dubovka

defensive fire quickly lost its intensity, and had died out completely within the hour. This meant that the Soviet bombers were able to strike enemy forces on the Stupeni-Dubovka and Telusha-Savichi roads, and in the woods nearby, with a high degree of accuracy from an altitude of 1200-1600 m (4000-5000 ft).

Elsewhere, attack aircraft delivered strikes on the leading vehicles of a panzer convoy north of Dubovka, groups of Il-2s and medium bombers succeeding each other over the target. There were so many aircraft in the immediate area that they had to queue up to make their attack runs. The convoy was soon blanketed in thick smoke and dust clouds, which made further attacks very difficult.

The 16th Air Army completed its strikes on the Bobruysk pocket after dark. In just a matter of hours, the encircled enemy forces had been on the receiving end of 1127 100- and 50-kg high-explosive bombs, 4897 25-, 10- and 8-kg fragmentation bombs, 5326 anti-tank bombs, 572 rocket projectiles, 27,880 cannon and 45,440 machine gun rounds. This weight of ordnance devastated German tanks, vehicles, anti-aircraft guns and troops alike. Later, a special commission of investigation determined that the aerial attacks southeast of Bobruysk had destroyed or damaged up to 150 tanks and assault guns, close to 1000 field/anti-aircraft guns, 300 trucks and 6000 vehicles. More than 1000 troops and 1500 horses had been killed.

Most importantly, this concentrated strike had completely disrupted the German command and control system in the area, resulting in total defeat for the enemy. Soldiers simply threw away their weapons, abandoned their equipment and fled into the forest. Some tried to cross the River Berezina to reach Bobruysk, but units of the 65th Army had already secured its western bank. The demoralised German force was finished off by 48th Army on 28 June. Bobruysk was liberated a day later.

MORE SUCCESSES

The 2nd Byelorussian Front's 49th Army had also been enjoying success during the Byelorussian offensive, having broken through enemy defensive lines in the Mogilev area on the very first day of the offensive on 23 June. Twenty-four hours later it had reached the River Basya, crossed it and secured a foothold on the other side. The front's mobile group was duly thrown into the gap and told to harass German forces until they commenced a front-wide retreat – the latter started on the night of 26 June, with withdrawing troops being pursued by the Soviet armies.

Having quickly realised that they could not defend Mogilev, the Germans had begun to withdraw heavy weapons and valuable equipment by rail as early as the 24th. Crews from 233rd and 230th ShADs, 4th Air Army, were immediately ordered to disrupt this operation by attacking 500 railway trucks that had been spotted at Shklov and Kopys stations. Following the capture of Mogilev on 28 June, an investigation commission sent into the town determined that the Il-2 attacks had put up to 25 per cent of the rolling stock at Shklov out of action.

Having lost Mogilev, the Germans now faced total defeat in Byelorussia. 1st and 3rd Byelorussian Fronts had crossed the Berezina and encircled the German Fourth Army east of Minsk. Every day until 3 July, Soviet aircraft harried the retreating enemy from the Dnieper to the Berezina. The effectiveness of Il-2 operations during this period was confirmed during the interrogation of German

This German Wespe self-propelled gun was destroyed in the Byelorussian forests by Il-2s in July 1944

prisoners of war ranging in rank from private to general officer. Gefreiter Frederick Alfred of the 3rd Company, 677th Railway Battalion, who was captured on 2 July, stated;

'German convoys travelling on the Orsha-Minsk highway turned south onto the Mogilev-Minsk road. On the forest roads we sustained constant strikes by Soviet attack aircraft and suffered terrible losses. Since vehicles proceeded in tightly packed rows of two to three at a time, losses often reached 50 to 60 per cent. I think that my convoy lost up to half of its strength to these air strikes. Our withdrawal routes were covered with thousands of destroyed vehicles and wagons, as well as with the bodies of horses and soldiers. The effect on morale was tremendous. When Soviet aircraft appeared overhead, the soldiers would abandon their vehicles and wagons and run for cover in the forest. Some vehicles would drive off the road, get stuck in swamps and create traffic jams.'

Gen Kurt von Tippelskirch, who had commanded the Fourth Army later wrote;

'Constant enemy air strikes caused heavy losses, and created non-stop jams in the retreating convoys. Russian attack aircraft destroyed crossings over the Berezina time and again, causing a large concentration of vehicles to build up on the eastern bank.'

The line of retreat took the Germans through marshy and wooded terrain with few roads. This meant that the *Wehrmacht* was forced to use two or three main roads, which were often jammed with three or even four rows of vehicles. At the same time, the Germans could not provide their retreating troops with anti-aircraft defence or fighter support. As a result, the Il-2s were able to operate in particularly favourable conditions. The retreating convoys had no chance of dispersing, while the Soviet attack aircraft constantly wheeled overhead, attacking at will.

The sorties flown on 29 June by units of 230th ShAD, commanded by Gen Getman, provide a good example of the operations undertaken by *Shturmovik* units at this time. Three groups of four Il-2s from 7th GShAP, led by Capts Ostapenko and Karabut and Sen Lt Demakov, took off at 0600 hrs to reconnoitre and attack retreating German forces. Each group was escorted by four La-5s from 229th IAD. Reaching Belynichi, the flight crews saw enemy vehicles, wagons and towed and horse-drawn artillery moving westwards.

The pilots spotted the largest concentration of enemy forces on the Zabolotie-Vasilevshchina road, with the head of the convoy approaching Pogost. When aerial photographs taken during the mission were subsequently examined, they revealed up to 600 vehicles on the road between there and Belynichi. All the bridges spanning the road and taking it over various rivers in the area were intact, and no movement was detected on smaller roads in the immediate area.

Il-2s from 4th Air Army dropped this bridge over the River Berezina, thus preventing German forces from retreating further west

Il-2s made several attack runs on the largest concentration of vehicles on the road between Zabolotie and Vasilevshchina. Acting on reconnaissance information, two more groups of four 7th GShAP Il-2s, led by Capt Demidov and Maj Ryabov, were ordered to attack at 0915 hrs. Groups of four to five Il-2s from other regiments in the division took off every eight to twenty minutes right up until 2030 hrs. And although the *Jagdwaffe* was virtually non-existent in the area, each group of Il-2s was escorted by a pair of fighters.

Between 1130 hrs and 1500 hrs, the attack aircraft destroyed every bridge on the Belynichi-Berezino road, bringing traffic to a standstill. A group of four Il-2s led by Capt Karabut was the first to deliver a precise strike on a bridge near Zapolie, together with a concentration of vehicles near it. These attacks forced the German convoys onto unmade tracks, which decreased their speed considerably and created even better targets for the Soviet aircraft.

A total of 40 groups of Il-2s flew combat sorties that day, and it was later determined that 230th ShAD's *Shturmovik* strikes had destroyed more than 100 vehicles. Additionally, some 500 tanks, self-propelled guns and towed artillery pieces were abandoned along a two-kilometre (1.25-mile) stretch of the Minsk highway 1.5 km northeast of Pogost.

Defeated and demoralised, German troops, who had retreated from the Dnieper under constant Soviet air attack, were unable to go on the defensive when they reached the River Berezina. Minsk was eventually liberated on 3 July when a 100,000-strong enemy force surrendered east of the city.

More German equipment destroyed by Il-2 attack aircraft on the 1st Byelorussian Front in July 1944

This defeat opened up a huge gap in Army Group Centre's defensive lines. To exploit it, on 4 July the Soviet Supreme High Command General Headquarters ordered that the right wing of the 1st Byelorussian Front should continue its advance towards Baranovichi and Brest, and secure bridgeheads on the western bank of the River Zapadniy

Bug. On the 8th, Soviet troops, with air support, broke the enemy resistance and captured the Baranovichi fortified area. Two days later they liberated Slonim. Providing close air support, 16th Air Army kept German forces west and northwest of Brest under constant attack from 28 June until 31 July.

On 28 July small groups of attack aircraft from 2nd GShAD and 299th ShAD, escorted by fighters, attacked encircled German forces near Bokhukaly and Kzhichev. Their first task was to strike the lead vehicles in a huge convoy of trucks, wagons, artillery pieces and infantry travelling towards Yanuv-Podlyaski. Each group of Il-2s picked its targets independently and bombed and strafed them in five to eight attack runs. With a lack of aerial resistance, escort fighters were able to join in too. The convoy was brought to a halt.

Most vehicles left the road, their drivers seeking cover in the forest and in the outskirts of populated areas. Many trucks got stuck in ditches, creating a traffic jam which made the retreating Germans even more vulnerable to air attack. All told that day, Soviet aircraft destroyed up to 600 vehicles, 30+ guns and up to 500 wagons, as well as slaughtering some 900 horses. It was also thought that as many as 1000 troops had been killed.

Over the following three days more strikes were launched against convoys travelling from Konstantynuv to Lositse that had been spotted by Lts Rossokhin and Milyukov of 59th GShAP, a further 400 vehicles and 200 wagons were destroyed. Two groups of six Il-2s headed by Maj Grebenkov were particularly successful. On 29 July they accounted for 45 vehicles, 40 wagons, two guns and up to 100 troops during two attack runs.

The encircled German forces west of Brest had lost battle-worthiness as a result of constant air attacks, and they were easily defeated by Soviet ground troops in various battles throughout July. An investigating commission was later to confirm the effectiveness of Soviet air strikes during the summer offensive in Byelorussia. Ground unit commanding officers also expressed their appreciation. One such message of gratitude reached Lt Col Lysenko, 218th ShAP CO, after he had led his Il-2s on a particularly effective strike on 28 July. 299th ShAD headquarters received the following communiqué later that same day;

'Your group of 11 Il-2s, which attacked enemy troops near Kzhichev (12 km west of Brest) did a splendid job. Express our gratitude to all flight crews. Col Boykov.'

Gen Turchinskiy, commander of 55th Guards Rifle Division, was a witness to the *Shturmoviks'* attack runs on this date, and he confirmed their 'exceptional efficiency', noting that his division was able to capture Konstantynuv with minimal resistance. There was also praise for 299th ShAD, whose attack aircraft provided air

CO of 15th GShAP, HSU Lt Col N I Svitenko is seen with his Il-2 in early 1944. Christened *Shchelkovskiy Shturmovik* ('Attacker from Shchelkovo'), the production costs involved in the construction of this aircraft had been met by Komsomol members of the Shchelkovskiy District Committee. Reaching 15th GShAP in the spring of 1943, the aircraft was flown by Lt Col Svitenko well into 1944

support to a mechanised cavalry group near Sedlets on the 30th. The unit's headquarters duly received the following message later in the day;

'To Gen Krupskiy. Mechanised cavalry group personnel greatly appreciate the outstanding work of your pilots near Sedlets. Soldiers and officers are very grateful for the close air support provided. Guards Lt Gen Kryukov, commander of the mechanised cavalry group.'

On 31 July Moscow recognised the success of the units which had liberated Sedlets and Minsk-Mazovetskiy. Under the order of the People's Commissar of Defence dated 19 August, 299th ShAD was transformed into 11th GShAD.

ACTION IN THE UKRAINE

Army Group Centre's defeat in Byelorussia, together with the successful offensive mounted by the Baltic and Leningrad Fronts against Army Group North and Army Group North Ukraine (the latter defeated in the Lvov-Sandomir area), created favourable conditions for follow-up attacks on enemy forces on the left flank of the Soviet-German Front. Under a plan devised by Supreme High Command General Headquarters, 2nd and 3rd Ukrainian Fronts were to breach enemy defensive lines northwest of Yassy and south of Tiraspol on 20 August. They were then to press on towards Khushi and Vasluy to encircle and destroy Army Group South Ukraine, which was defending the Kishinev salient.

With the Germans having established a well-fortified defence in depth based on the River Dniester, the Soviet command decided against ordering a preliminary air bombardment in this area. Instead, it chose to focus the main efforts of 5th and 17th Air Armies on providing overwhelming close air support for the attacks launched by 27th, 52nd, 37th and 36th Armies on the German River Dniester defences. Attack aircraft and bombers were also expected to support the 6th Tank Army and the 4th and 7th Mechanised Corps, which were to be committed to achieving a breakthrough in the River Dniester area. Some 7980 combat sorties were expected to be flown on the first three days of the offensive.

Of all the Il-2 units committed to this huge offensive, 2nd ShAK stood out through its provision of exceptional close air support to 27th Army on the main axis of advance. Led by Gen V V Stepichev, the unit garnered great praise for the planning, organisation and execution of the myriad combat sorties that it undertook. Indeed, a number of the missions flown by 2nd ShAK were included in every air tactics textbook produced in the USSR well into the post-war years.

During the breakthrough, 2nd ShAK aircraft were to either attack pre-determined targets or silence artillery and mortar batteries that betrayed their positions following the Red Army's preparatory bombardment. The unit's chief

Lt Gen V V Stepichev, CO of 2nd GShAK, delivers a speech during a ceremony to mark the awarding of the Guards title to the corps and 232nd ShAD in October 1944

objective, however, was to deal with pockets of resistance along the main line of advance.

A total of 480 Il-2 combat sorties were planned by 2nd ShAK for the first day of the offensive, which meant an average of 2.4 sorties for every attack aircraft. In order for this to be achieved, the Soviet command ensured that a high density of *Shturmoviks* were committed to the campaign – 32 per frontline kilometre in the area of the breakthrough. With such numbers involved in the offensive, 2nd ShAK was expected to retain a constant presence over the battlefield.

Every 27th Army unit detailed signalmen to fire flares once Il-2s were overhead, thus marking the position of friendly troops. 2nd ShAK's command post was to warn the signalmen of approaching Soviet ground attack aircraft via the ground units' liaison officers. If no such warning was given, the signalmen were to fire flares towards the enemy positions on their own initiative as the Il-2s neared them.

Special attention was paid to cooperation between 2nd ShAK and artillery units, with each having assigned targets. For instance, the attack aircraft flew only reconnaissance missions during the preliminary bombardment, while the gunners were ordered to silence enemy defensive emplacements. After the preparatory bombardment, artillery units were to focus on establishing a two-layer barrage directly in front of the advancing Soviet tanks and infantry. Meanwhile, the Il-2s were to attack enemy strongpoints and troops behind the artillery barrage. As the gunners changed their firing positions, *Shturmovik* sorties were to be stepped up to maintain the pressure on the enemy.

Flight crews conducted thorough pre-flight briefings, studying the operations area to which they had been assigned and familiarising themselves with the artillery firing times. They even considered the range and trajectories of the shells that would be fired, preparing diagrams based on the calibre of the rounds and the location of the batteries.

When it came time for the gunners to designate targets for the attack aircraft, the front artillery commander allocated a howitzer battery to be located within the Il-2 operations area and provided with a direct telephone line to the air corps commander's observation post. When the *Shturmoviks* approached the battlefield, the gunners were to fire on Gen Stepichev's orders so as to clearly indicate the targets to the aircrew.

Il-2 PHOTO-FLIGHTS

Although non-stop aerial reconnaissance flights were made on the eve of the offensive in the Yassy and the Kishinev areas, senior Soviet commanders were not quite satisfied with the quality of the aerial photographs being taken from Pe-2s performing these missions. The chief of 2nd ShAK's aerial photographic reconnaissance unit suggested that several Il-2s be fitted with four synchronised AFA-IM cameras to take oblique photographs from an altitude of 20-50 m (65-160 ft). Modified *Shturmoviks* duly flew a total of 24 group oblique photographic sorties over 20 days in August.

On such flights, a pair of camera-equipped Il-2s would typically be supported by four to six aircraft tasked with suppressing anti-aircraft defences and six to eight escort fighters. The Il-2 reconnaissance aircraft managed to photograph the entire forward edge of the battle area, all intermediate positions and fortified areas and all roads and rivers from Yassy and Tyrgu-Frumos. The total area of coverage was 790 sq km (305 sq miles), and not a single aircraft was lost during the operation.

These sorties paid particular attention to photographing the axis of advance for friendly armour. Each unit received a panoramic photograph covering an area 10 km (six miles) directly ahead of it. They were studied by all officers and tank drivers, and the imagery enabled the crews to carry out their assigned combat tasks precisely and on time, as they knew in advance what natural and man-made obstacles to expect.

Sen Lt Nikitin, Lt Klevtsov and Capts Palagin and Samodelkin distinguished themselves during aerial photography missions. Their Il-2s often returned to base peppered with bullet holes, yet these pilots, and a handful of others, continued to fly dangerous photographic sorties.

Thanks to the reconnaissance data gained by the Il-2s, 2nd Ukrainian Front command correctly decided that German forces were in a weakened state overall. Now was the right time to launch the Yassy-Kishinev offensive.

The guns opened up with a preliminary 90-minute bombardment at 0610 hrs on 20 August. Il-2 reconnaissance aircraft had taken off ten minutes prior to the barrage ending so as to monitor the roads leading to the breakthrough area. Their photographs and verbal reports would be critical when it came to determining whether the enemy was moving in reserves or retreating. The first pair of Il-2 reconnaissance aircraft appeared over the battlefield at 0630 hrs, and during the course of their mission they flew along every road in the breakthrough area to a depth of up to 30 km (19 miles). They failed to detect any movement.

As previously planned, during the first four hours of the offensive, 2nd ShAK delivered continuous air strikes. Groups of 16-20 Il-2s made four to five attack runs, staying over the battlefield for 20 or more minutes. The first group of 20 Il-2s from 131st GShAP, 7th GShAD, led by regimental CO Maj Davydov, appeared over the battlefield at 0720 hrs and attacked artillery positions four kilometres (2.5 miles) northeast of Podul-Ioaley. The Soviet attack aircraft made their first runs individually, before forming a circle and carrying out three more runs over the next 15 minutes. Soviet infantry and tanks launched a simultaneous attack, with the guns laying down a powerful barrage in front of the advancing tanks, which formed the spearhead. The latter were followed by self-propelled guns, some 200-300 m behind.

As the first group of attack aircraft made their final runs, the second group of 15 Il-2s from 130th GShAP, 7th GShAD, led by regimental CO Lt Col Greben, closed in on their target. Another 20 Il-2s appeared over the battlefield at 0742 hrs, being joined 27 minutes later by three more groups of 14, eight and 12 Il-2s, respectively, from 2nd ShAK. Then, at 0812 hrs

Air gunner Vladimir Zagainov (left) and flight crew commander HSU Sen Lt M E Nikitin of 131st GShAP, 7th GshAD, smile for the camera after a combat sortie during the Yassy-Kishinev Operation in August 1944

Pilots and air gunners of 131st GShAP, 7th GShAD, 2nd ShAK are briefed for a combat mission during the Yassy-Kishinev Operation in August 1944

and 0837 hrs, two more groups totalling 16 Il-2s turned up, with another 20 aircraft striking at 0855 hrs. There was little respite for the enemy, as 45 minutes later 15 Il-2s attacked artillery and mortar batteries. At 1000 hrs the German guns sustained another blow, dealt by 14 more Il-2s. Two more groups of seven and eight *Shturmoviks* attacked at 1018 hrs and 1042 hrs. To complete the first stage of the breakthrough, 16 Il-2s swooped down at 1045 hrs. Soviet Il-2s had carried out virtually non-stop attacks for the first three-and-a-half

hours of the offensive, thus preventing enemy troops from regaining the defensive positions they had vacated during the artillery bombardment.

By 1130 hrs a wedge some 5-6 km (3-4 miles) deep had been driven into the German defensive line. Soviet infantry and tank units had quickly reached the River Vakhluy and captured a 50-ton pontoon bridge near Khostshesht. By that time the breach had been increased to eight kilometres (five miles).

After their initial attacks the Il-2s operated in groups of eight to twelve aircraft, their mission tasking being based on information from air corps command posts and air reconnaissance data. If an Il-2 group remained too long over the battlefield and interfered with the succeeding group, Stepichev would order it to abort its attack and withdraw.

The attacks on enemy defensive positions mounted by 2nd ShAK were particularly effective on 20 August. Between 0837 hrs and 0855 hrs, Lt Col Melnikov, CO of 570th ShAP, 231st ShAD, led 20 Il-2s in an attack on artillery and mortar batteries sited up to three kilometres from the forward edge of the battle area.

Melnikov's aircraft formed into columns of four and approached the target from the right. In an effort to conceal the true course of their attack from the enemy, the first group of four Il-2s (flown by the most experienced pilots) proceeded in a right echelon formation, while other groups followed them in a left echelon formation. The groups of four Il-2s were spaced 300 m apart. When German guns were detected, Melnikov gave the order to attack. The first run was made from the northeast out of the sun at an altitude of 1000 m (3000 ft), with the groups in line ahead.

After the first run, they formed four-aircraft circles, with each group attacking independently. In four attack runs, Melnikov's group first fired rockets before dropping their bombs and then raking the targets with their guns. Whilst conducting these attack runs, a specially-detailed group of four Il-2s made sure the anti-aircraft gunners kept their heads down. According to reports by flight crews, backed up by their on-board cameras, the air strike destroyed three mortar pits and two field artillery batteries. They also suppressed a flak battery and badly damaged three assault guns.

Group leader Mikhail Chekurin of 92nd GShAP briefs pilots on a forthcoming combat mission on the 1st Ukrainian Front in August 1944. These men are (from left to right) Nikolay Lezhnev, Didenko, unidentified, unidentified, Timchenko, Mikhail Chekurin, Sergey Ryabov, Ivan Glebov and Nikolay Sviridov

Capt Yury S Afanasiev of 154th GShAP, 307th ShAD, 3rd ShAK poses in the autumn of 1944 with his Il-2 which displayed the inscription *Za Borisa* ('For Boris') on its left side. Afanasiev had this tribute to Boris Kononov painted onto his aircraft after his flight leader had been killed in action

The pilot of this Il-2 from 92nd GShAP bailed out after his aircraft was hit by flak

Six Fw 190s tried to intercept the Il-2s during their second attack run, but well-coordinated defensive fire from the air gunners proved highly effective. Sen Sgt Abramov shot down one of the fighters, causing the rest to flee without attempting another attack on the Soviet aircraft.

To provide the Il-2s with continuous command and control information, the forward observation posts had advanced alongside the rifle units' command posts. Manned by liaison officers with VHF/UHF radio sets, these observation posts represented a crucial factor in Gen Stepichev's ability to control the movements of his attack aircraft as the battle developed. The Il-2s were now able to deliver accurate attacks immediately ahead of the advancing ground forces thanks to the development of a highly-organised command and control system.

Its effectiveness was well illustrated by Lt Col Bykov and the Il-2s of the 167th GShAD that he led over the battlefield at 1045 hrs on 20 August. Soviet ground troops had been halted by heavy enemy fire east of Totoeschiy, and Stepichev radioed Bykov's group to suppress the enemy strongpoint that was holding up the advance. Their task was complicated by the fact that the German emplacements were just 200 m from the attacking forces, but the Red Army soldiers were able to provide accurate target designation through the use of signal flares. Adopting a circular formation, the Soviet aircraft made four accurate attack runs, after which the enemy weapons stopped firing and the Soviet advance was able to continue. Bykov's group was commended for its action.

During the early hours of the offensive, 2nd ShAK flew a total of 217 combat sorties. At 1200 hrs, reconnaissance aircraft reported that the enemy was beginning to retreat. Although there had been no requests for close air support from ground units, and despite the battlefield being obscured by a cloud of dust reaching up to 400-500 m (1300-1600 ft), Stepichev detailed every available aircraft to attack the retreating convoys. Some 20 groups of eight to sixteen Il-2s flew 201 combat sorties between 1205 hrs and 1912 hrs.

A group of seven Il-2s from 570th ShAP, 231st ShAD, led by Lt Strobykin, dropped 20 ZAB-100-65TSh incendiary bombs – each carried 65 thermite balls – on a German convoy in the Voyneshti, Forleshti and Lugani areas from an altitude of 400-1000 m. Subsequent investigation by a special commission, analysis of photos and

This bridge over the River Prut also fell victim to marauding Il-2s in 1944

Il-2s of 8th GPShAP, Black Sea Fleet Air Force, taxi out prior to taking off on the Novorossiysk Front in August 1943. The three red stars displayed on the fin tip of the aircraft closest to the camera indicate that its crew had shot down three German aircraft. The inscription on the *Shturmovik's* fuselage reads *Za chest Gvardii* ('To the honour of the Guards'), which was a favourite battle cry amongst Guards units

information from the local population revealed that the strike had left 15 enemy vehicles burnt out and about 150 soldiers dead. In fact, the Il-2 air strikes on retreating troops completely disrupted the German command and control system and the deployment of reserves, facilitating the Soviet advances.

Efficient radio communications and command and control played a great part in this success. Eight Il-2s from 568th ShAP, 231st ShAD that were led by Capt Lozorenko and assigned to detect and attack retreating enemy convoys, encountered another pair from the same division, headed by Lt Frolov, returning from a reconnaissance mission. Frolov radioed Lozorenko with information about a large convoy moving south of the River Bakhluy. It was immediately attacked by Lozorenko's Il-2s. Having exhausted their weaponry and turned for home, the group met Lt Agrb's Il-2s, whose pilots had similar orders. Lozorenko passed on the convoy's coordinates so that Agrb's group could mount a second attack on the vehicles, which then ground to a halt and were finished off by 6th Tank Army.

2nd ShAK's air reconnaissance missions during this time were also highly effective. The aircraft normally operated in groups of two to six, escorted by up to four La-5s. They monitored the enemy from low-level up to 1000 m, attacking the most crucial targets from dawn until dusk. The unit's headquarters received reconnaissance information within 20-30 minutes of the flight returning to base, and then passed it to the air army headquarters.

By 1900 hrs on 20 August, Soviet armies had reached Syrka, Doroshkani, Kukuteni and Urikaniy, while 6th Tank Army units had fought their way through to Peusheshti and Golmiluy. Within 12 hours of launching the offensive, 27th Army and 6th Tank Army had opened up two breaches in the enemy defensive line and seized the Podul-Iloaey stronghold. The power and efficiency of Il-2 operations had played a key part in this success. Under interrogation a captured German officer said;

'When the preparatory bombardment was over we thought we could recover and repulse the Russian infantry and tanks, but attack aircraft appeared overhead and gave us no chance to recover. They forced us to

leave our equipment and run for it. The attack aircraft were constantly wheeling overhead. It was horrible.'

According to other German prisoners, the preliminary bombardment and the air strikes on 20 August killed up to half the personnel manning the first defensive line. Losses among officers were even higher. A captured officer from the 76th Infantry Division stated that the regiments in his division had lost up to 80 per cent of their officers on the first day.

The Rumanian Third Army ceased resistance on 24 August, when Rumania declared war on Germany. An encircled enemy force east of the River Prut was destroyed three days later.

Those German units which had managed to cross the Prut southwest of Khushi were defeated on the 29th. This had resulted in the complete annihilation of Army Group South Ukraine, with the destruction of 22 German divisions and all the Rumanian ones, plus the collapse of the German defence in the southern wing of the Soviet-German Front.

By order of the People's Commissar of Defence, dated 27 October 1944, 2nd ShAK, which had particularly distinguished itself during the operation, became 3rd GShAK. 231st ShAD also received the Guards title to become 12th GShAD. They were the last attack aircraft regiments and divisions to receive the coveted Guards title during the Great Patriotic War, and along with the remaining Guards Il-2 units, they continued to take the fight to the enemy until VE-Day.

There were also two naval aviation guards attack aircraft regiments created, namely 7th and 8th GPShAPs. 7th GPShAP had previously been 57th Dive-Bomber Air Regiment of the Red-Banner Baltic Fleet Air Force, which had distinguished itself during the Battle of Leningrad. 8th GPShAP had been 18th ShAP of the Black Sea Fleet Air Force, which received the Guards title for the heroism it displayed in the battles for Sevastopol, Novorossiysk and the Taman Peninsula. Both regiments received their titles by order of the People's Commissar of the Navy dated 1 March 1943.

From their poorly-organised attempt to stem German advances into the Soviet Union in 1941, Il-2 units had been transformed into a highly effective airborne artillery capable of operating with pinpoint accuracy against enemy strong points ahead of advancing forces. Through hard-won combat experience in the dark days of 1941-42, the *Shturmovik* had evolved into the scourge of the *Wehrmacht's* once vaunted panzer units.

Although Il-2 units had made a major contribution to the defeat of the invading armies, only a comparative handful were to have their exploits recognised through the receipt of the coveted Guards title. They were rightly regarded by the Red Army Air Force as being the best of the best.

A German coaster is strafed by an Il-2 from 7th GShAP, Red-Banner Baltic Fleet Air Force on 8 June 1944

16th Air Army Il-2s fly in close formation over the devastated streets of Berlin shortly after German forces surrendered to Soviet troops in May 1945

APPENDICES

GUARDS ATTACK AIRCRAFT UNITS

Regiments

6th Moscow Red Banner Guards Attack Aircraft Regiment (6/12/41)

7th Sevastopol Red Banner Guards Attack Aircraft Regiment (7/3/42)

15th Neva Red Banner Guards Attack Aircraft Regiment (7/3/42)

17th Guards Attack Aircraft Regiment (7/3/42)

33rd Voronezh Red Banner Guards Attack Aircraft Regiment (22/11/43)

43rd Volkovysk Red Banner Guards Attack Aircraft Regiment (8/2/43)

58th Don Red Banner Guards Attack Aircraft Regiment (8/2/43)

59th Baranovichi Red Banner Guards Attack Aircraft Regiment (8/2/43)

70th Byelorussian Red Banner Guards Attack Aircraft Regiment (18/3/43)

71st Radomsk Red Banner Guards Attack Aircraft Regiment (18/3/43)

74th Stalingrad Red Banner Guards Attack Aircraft Regiment (18/3/43)

75th Stalingrad Red Banner Guards Attack Aircraft Regiment (18/3/43)

76th Melitopol Red Banner Guards Attack Aircraft Regiment (18/3/43)

78th Volga Red Banner Guards Attack Aircraft Regiment (18/3/43)

79th Mozyr Guards Attack Aircraft Regiment (18/3/43)

90th Starokonstantinov Red Banner Guards Attack Aircraft Regiment (1/5/43)

91st Vladimir-Volynskiy Red Banner Guards Attack Aircraft Regiment (1/5/43)

92nd Kamenets-Podolskiy Guards Attack Aircraft Regiment (1/5/43)

93rd Rava-Russkiy Guards Attack Aircraft Regiment (1/5/43)

94th Vladimir-Volynskiy Guards Attack Aircraft Regiment (1/5/43)

95th Rava-Russkiy Red Banner Guards Attack Aircraft Regiment (1/5/43)

108th Rava-Russkiy Guards Attack Aircraft Regiment (24/8/43)

109th Vladimir-Volynskiy Guards Attack Aircraft Regiment (24/8/43)

110th Vistula Guards Attack Aircraft Regiment (24/8/43)

118th Kursk Guards Attack Aircraft Regiment (3/9/43)

130th Bratislava Red Banner Guards Attack Aircraft Regiment (3/9/43)

131st Budapest Guards Attack Aircraft Regiment (3/9/43)

132nd Guards Attack Aircraft Regiment (3/9/43)

136th Stalin Red Banner Guards Attack Aircraft Regiment (23/10/43)

140th Kiev Red Banner Guards Attack Aircraft Regiment (5/2/44)

141st Sandomir Red Banner Guards Attack Aircraft Regiment (5/2/44)

142nd Sandomir Guards Attack Aircraft Regiment (5/2/44)

143rd Lvov Guards Attack Aircraft Regiment (5/2/44)

144th Lvov Guards Attack Aircraft Regiment (5/2/44)

154th Orsha Red Banner Guards Attack Aircraft Regiment (14/4/44)

155th Kiev Red Banner Guards Attack Aircraft Regiment (5/2/44)

165th Stanislav Red Banner Guards Attack Aircraft Regiment (5/2/44)

166th Red Banner Guards Attack Aircraft Regiment (5/2/44)

167th Starokonstantinov Guards Attack Aircraft Regiment (5/2/44)

173rd Sloutsk Red Banner Guards Attack Aircraft Regiment (19/8/44)

174th Sloutsk Red Banner Guards Attack Aircraft Regiment (19/8/44)

175th Sloutsk Red Banner Guards Attack Aircraft Regiment (19/8/44)

187th Red Banner Guards Attack Aircraft Regiment (27/10/44)

188th Budapest Guards Attack Aircraft Regiment (27/10/44)

189th Brest Guards Attack Aircraft Regiment (27/10/44)

190th Budapest Guards Attack Aircraft Regiment (27/10/44)

7th Tallinn Naval Aviation Red-Banner Guards Dive Attack Aircraft Regiment (1/3/43)

8th Feodosiya Naval Aviation Twice Red-Banner Guards Attack Aircraft Regiment (1/3/43)

Divisions

1st Stalingrad Twice Red Banner Guards Attack Aircraft Division (18/3/43)

2nd Chernigov-Rechitsk Red Banner Guards Attack Aircraft Division (18/3/43)

3rd Valdai-Kovel Red Banner Guards Attack Aircraft Division (18/3/43)

4th Kiev Red Banner Guards Attack Aircraft Division (1/5/43)

5th Zaporozhie Red Banner Guards Attack Aircraft Division (1/5/43)

6th Zaporozhie Twice Red Banner Guards Attack Aircraft Division (24/8/43)

7th Debrecen Red Banner Guards Attack Aircraft Division (3/9/43)

8th Poltava Red Banner Guards Attack Aircraft Division (5/2/44)

9th Krasnograd Red Banner Guards Attack Aircraft Division (5/2/44)

10th Voronezh-Kiev Red Banner Guards Attack Aircraft Division (5/2/44)

11th Nezhinsk Red Banner Guards Attack Aircraft Division (19/8/44)

12th Roslavl Red Banner Guards Attack Aircraft Division (27/10/44)

Corps

1st Kirovograd-Berlin Red Banner Guards Attack Aircraft Corps (5/2/44)

2nd Vladimir-Volyn Red Banner Guards Attack Aircraft Corps (28/9/44)

3rd Smolensk-Budapest Red Banner Guards Attack Aircraft Corps (27/10/44)

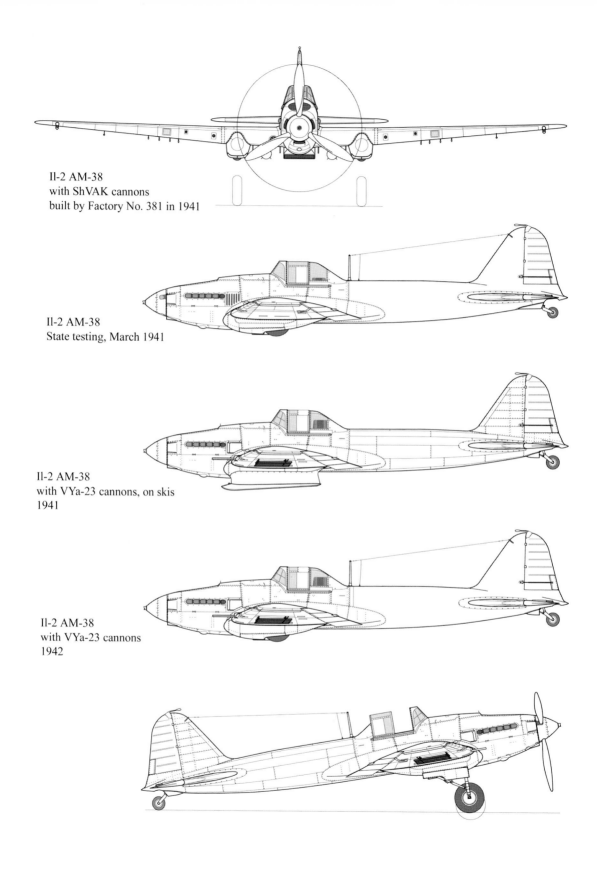

Il-2 AM-38
with ShVAK cannons
built by Factory No. 381 in 1941

Il-2 AM-38
State testing, March 1941

Il-2 AM-38
with VYa-23 cannons, on skis
1941

Il-2 AM-38
with VYa-23 cannons
1942

0   1   2   3

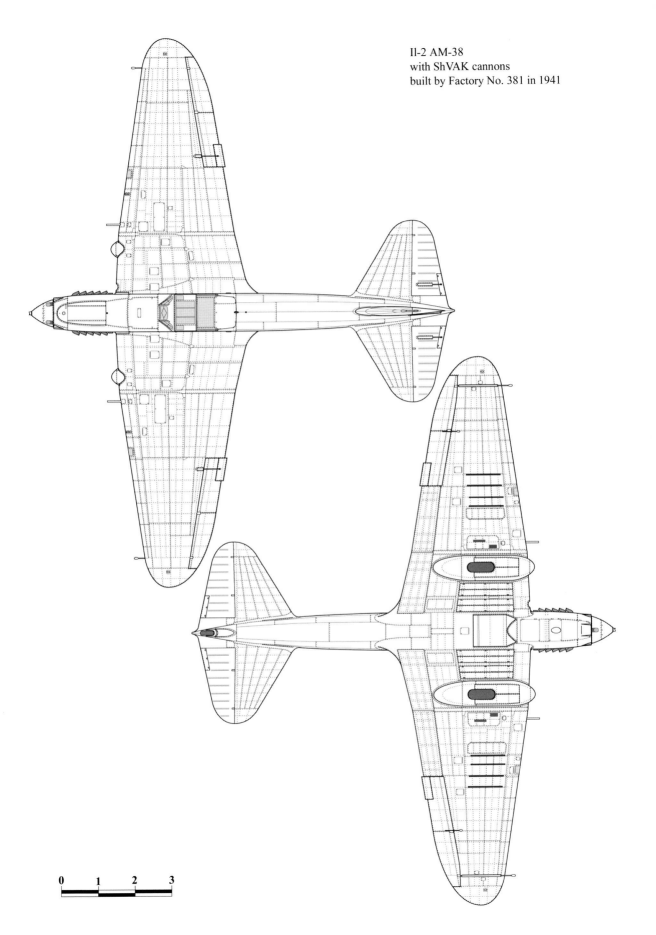

Il-2 AM-38
with ShVAK cannons
built by Factory No. 381 in 1941

0   1   2   3

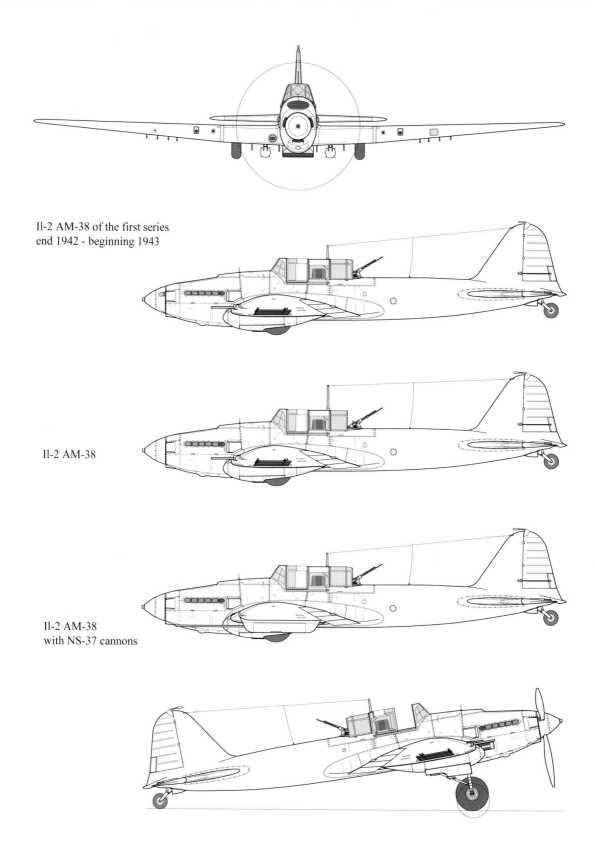

Il-2 AM-38 of the first series
end 1942 - beginning 1943

Il-2 AM-38

Il-2 AM-38
with NS-37 cannons

0   1   2   3

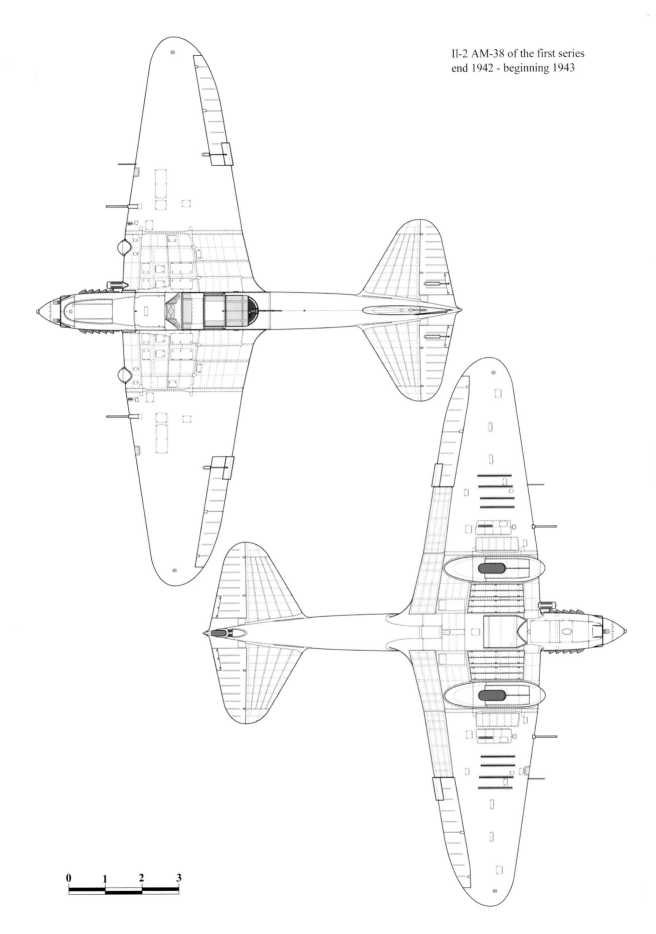

Il-2 AM-38 of the first series
end 1942 - beginning 1943

0   1   2   3

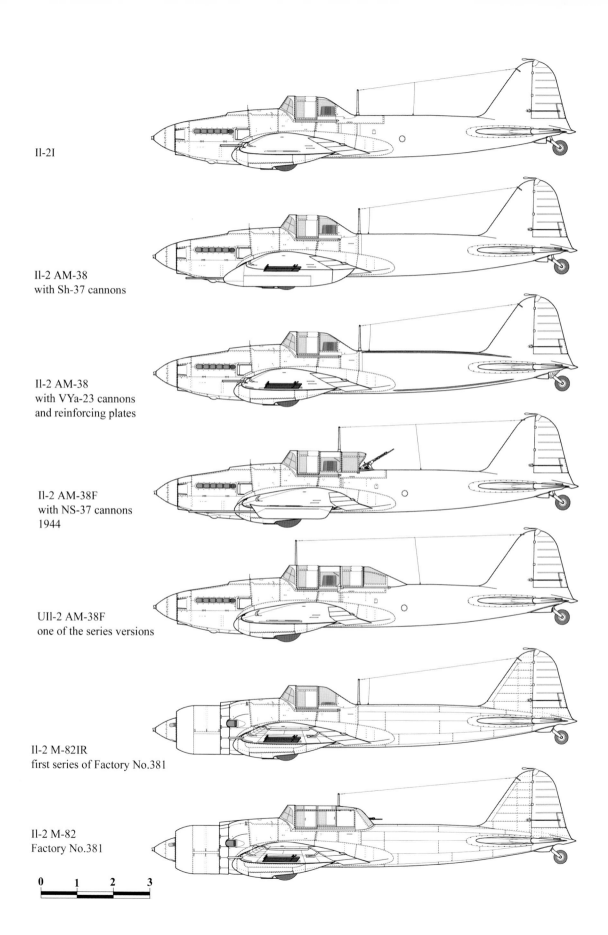

Il-2I

Il-2 AM-38
with Sh-37 cannons

Il-2 AM-38
with VYa-23 cannons
and reinforcing plates

Il-2 AM-38F
with NS-37 cannons
1944

UIl-2 AM-38F
one of the series versions

Il-2 M-82IR
first series of Factory No.381

Il-2 M-82
Factory No.381

0   1   2   3

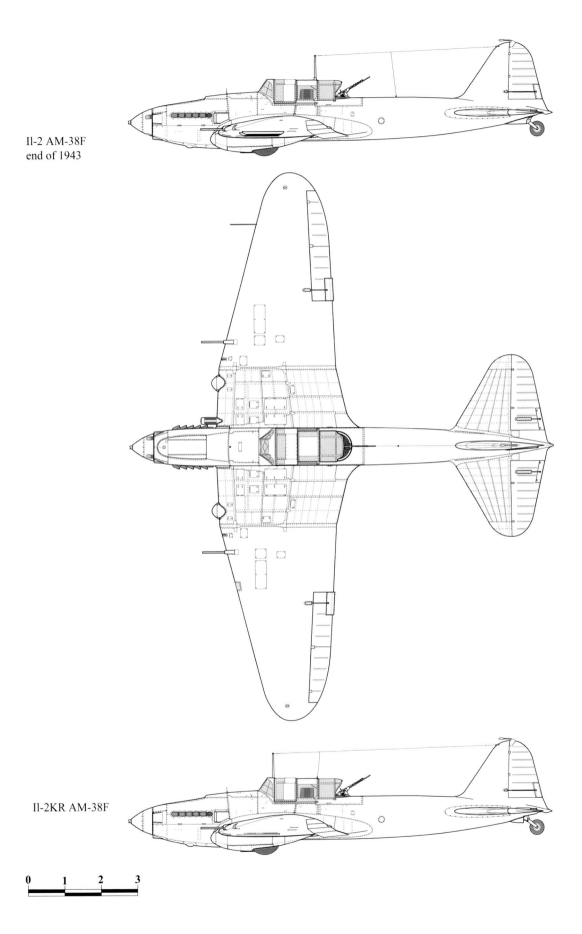

Il-2 AM-38F
end of 1943

Il-2KR AM-38F

0   1   2   3

COLOUR PLATES

1

Il-2 of 174th ShAP, Leningrad Front, September 1941
This regiment distinguished itself during attacks on Bf 109Fs assigned to *Jagdgeschwader* 54 based at Krasnogvardeysk and Siverskaya airfields in November 1941 and spring 1942. The regiment became 15th GShAP by Order No 70 of the People's Commissar of Defence, dated 7 March 1942. On 1 May 1943 it received the honorary title of 'Nevskiy' for air combat over the Neva area.

2

Il-2 of 7th GShAP, Southern Front, March 1942
Displaying the inscription *Smert Fashistskim Okkupantam* ('Death to Fascist Invaders') on its fuselage, this aircraft was routinely flown by squadron leader Maj N A Zub, who became famous for his pinpoint attacks on enemy troops and equipment. Later made CO of 210th ShAP, Zub was killed over the Blue Line on 22 July 1943 whilst flying his 382nd combat sortie in two years of constant fighting in the frontline. He was posthumously awarded the title of HSU.

3

Il-2 of 505th ShAP, Stalingrad sector, December 1942
Together with other regiments of 226th ShAD that had distinguished themselves in the dogged defence of Stalingrad, 505th ShAP became 75th GShAP with the issuing of Order No 128 of the People's Commissar of Defence on 18 March 1943 – the division itself became 1st GShAD. This aircraft was often flown by Sgt Musa G Gareev during the winter defence of Stalingrad. A veteran Il-2 pilot, Gareev later became a twice HSU.

4

Il-2 of 504th ShAP, Stalingrad area, December 1942
Also seeing much action over Stalingrad in 1942-43, 504th ShAP became 74th GShAP on 18 March 1943 during Order No 128 issued by the People's Commissar of Defence decree on 18 March 1943. Sen Lt Borodin was one of the unit's most courageous pilots, being awarded the title of HSU for his part in air operations over the River Volga in 1942-43.

5

Il-2 of 667th ShAP, Kalinin Front, January 1943
The members of Moscow-based Yaroslavl Komsomol Factory No 30 bought a whole squadron of Il-2s, and the suitably decorated aircraft were in turn handed over to the best pilots of 667th ShAP, 292nd ShAD, 1st ShAK in early 1943. The regiment became 141st GShAP in Order 016 of the People's Commissar of Defence, dated 5 February 1944.

6

Il-2 of 667th ShAP, Kalinin Front, January 1943
667th ShAP was designated as the frontline service trials unit for the two-seat Il-2 in late 1942. This particular aircraft was amongst those bought by Yaroslavl Komsomol Factory No 30, the Il-2 being decorated with *Yaroslavskiy Komsomolets* titling in a similar style to that seen on the single-seat *Shturmoviks* that were also flown by the unit at this time.

7

Il-2 of 15th GShAP, Leningrad Front, 1943
Christened *Shchelkovskiy Shturmovik* ('Attacker from Shchelkovo'), this Il-2's production costs were met by Komsomol members of the Shchelkovskiy District Committee. Reaching 15th GShAP in the spring of 1943 and remaining in service well into 1944, the aircraft was flown by unit CO Lt Col N I Svitenko, who was also a HSU.

8

Il-2 of 15th GShAP, Leningrad Front, 1943
Also assigned to 15th GShAP in the spring of 1943, this Il-2 sported lion artwork, applied by the regimental artist, on both sides of its fin. The regiment was attached to 277th ShAD, 13th Air Army at this time. Between 12-30 January 1943, 15th GShAP pilots had distinguished themselves during Operation *Iskra*, when the German forces of Army Group North were crushed in a Red Army vice between 57th Army (Leningrad Front) and 2nd Shock Army (Volkhov Front). The Soviets' *Iskra* victory breached the long-standing German blockade of Leningrad.

9

Il-2 of 820th ShAP, Kharkov Front, May 1943
This aircraft, piloted by Sgt Zakharov of 820th ShAP, suffered heavy damage whilst attacking Kharkov-Sokolniki airfield on 6 May 1943, although it was subsequently repaired. 820th ShAP later became 155th GShAP with the issuing of Order 016 by the People's Commissar of Defence on 5 February 1944.

10

Il-2 of 76th GShAP, Kotelnikovo, summer 1943
As mentioned in the commentary for Plate 3, following the division's exploits in the Battle of Stalingrad, 226th ShAD became 1st GShAD on 18 March 1943. Divisional regiments also received the title of Guards regiments, with 504th ShAP being transformed into 74th GShAP, 505th ShAP into 75th GShAP and 225th ShAP into 76th GShAP. All three regiments had suffered heavy losses during combat operations over the Volga River in the defence of Stalingrad, and they had received personnel and materiel reinforcements in March 1943. Amongst the aircraft supplied to 76th GShAP

was this two-seat Il-2, built at Factory No 18 in Kuybyshev and ferried to the regimental base in Kotelnikovo. The *Shturmovik* was assigned to newly-promoted Lt Musa G Gareev, who had previously flown with 505th ShAP. A highly experienced attack pilot, he would see much action in this aircraft during the summer 1943 offensive launched by the Southern Front that was aimed at breaking through enemy defensive lines on the Mius River. Lt Gareev shot down two German fighters in air engagements during the course of the offensive, Red Army ground units, which saw the Luftwaffe fighters crash officially confirming his victories. On 1 August Gareev's long-lived Il-2 'Yellow 31' was hit by anti-aircraft artillery and then attacked by enemy fighters near the Garany River. The *Shturmovik's* oil radiator caught fire, its cockpit armour was pierced, the pilot's instrument panel was destroyed, air gunner Sgt A I Kiryanov was wounded and, finally, the engine started to fail. However, Gareev managed to cross the Mius River and belly-land the heavily damaged aircraft. On seeing the Il-2 come down, the enemy targeted it with a heavy artillery barrage until it was destroyed.

11

Il-2 of 8th GPShAP, Novorossiysk Front, August 1943

Bearing the inscription *Za Rodinu!* ('For Motherland!') on the right side of its fuselage and *Za chest Gvardii* ('To the honour of the Guards') on the left side, this aircraft was assigned to 8th GPShAP of the Black Sea Fleet Air Force. One of only two Naval Aviation Il-2 units to achieve Guards status, 8th GPShAP had previously been 18th ShAP of the Black Sea Fleet Air Force, and it had received the Guards title for the heroism its crews had displayed in the battles for Sevastopol, Novorossiysk and the Taman Peninsula in 1942. The regiment's title was announced with the issuing of Order No 79 by the People's Commissar of the Navy on 1 March 1943.

12

Il-2 of 8th GPShAP, Novorossiysk Front, August 1943

The three red stars displayed on the fin tip of this 8th GPShAP Il-2 indicate that its crew had shot down three German aircraft. The inscription on the *Shturmovik's* fuselage reads *Za chest Gvardii* ('To the honour of the Guards'), which was a favourite battle cry amongst Guards units.

13

Il-2 of 8th GPShAP, Saki, April 1944

Although the Black Sea Fleet Air Force was also equipped with both conventional medium bombers and dedicated torpedo-bombers, attack aircraft regiments provided the bulk of its strike force in spring 1944. This camouflaged Il-2 from 8th GPShAP was based at Saki airfield, in the Crimea, during the Battle of Sevastopol in April-May 1944.

14

Il-2 of 7th GShAP, North Caucasus Front, summer 1943

The aircraft displays the standard 1943 three-colour camouflage finish seen on most Il-2s, as well as a slanting white stripe on its vertical tail for quick identification purposes of 7th GShAP aircraft when in flight.

15

Il-2 of 7th GShAP, North Caucasus Front, August 1943

Regimental artist Aleksandr Bulyndenko painted a musical emblem on the aircraft flown by HSU Capt V B Emelyanenko, who had been a composer with the Moscow Conservatory pre-war. Continuing the musical theme once in uniform, Emelyanenko had taken a balalaika with him when posted to 7th GShAP.

16

Il-2 of 617th ShAP, Kharkov Front, August 1943

Flown by Jnr Lt V P Aleksukhin and air gunner A D Gatayunov, this aircraft displays the inscription *Aleksandr Suvorov* and a representation of the famous Russian military leader painted on the tail. Aleksukhin and Gatayunov distinguished themselves during the Battle of Kursk when they performed several dozen sorties hunting for enemy troop trains and vehicles. 617th ShAP subsequently became 167th GShAP with the issuing of Order 018 on 5 February 1944 by the People's Commissar of Defence following the regiment's exploits in the Battle of Kursk.

17

Il-2 of 15th GShAP, Leningrad Front, June 1944

This single-seat Il-2 of 15th GShAP featured a non-standard camouflage paint scheme used during Operation *Vyborg* on the Leningrad Front in June 1944. It was one of only a handful of single-seat Il-2s to survive into 1944, with most units having by then switched over to two-seat *Shturmoviks*.

18

Il-2 of 90th GShAP, 1st Ukrainian Front, autumn 1944

Having distinguished itself when designated 671st ShAP during combat operations near Velikie Luki and Rzhev in the winter of 1942-43, 90th GShAP helped support units of the 1st Ukrainian Front when they crossed the Vistula River and tried to secure the Sandomir foothold in the autumn of 1944. Pilots from 90th GShAP, along with other flight crews from 4th GShAD, 5th ShAK, effectively operated as the long-range artillery for Red Army troops, providing them with virtually round-the-clock close air support as they fended off a series of fierce counterattacks by German panzers. This aircraft was one of the *Shturmoviks* that saw considerable action during the defence of the Sandomir foothold.

19

Il-2 of 8th GPShAP, Crimea, April 1944
Most Il-2s flown by 8th GPShAP of the Black Sea Fleet Air Force bore inscriptions on their fuselages, and this aircraft was no exception to that rule. Assigned to regiment CO and twice HSU Lt Col N V Chelnokov, the *Shturmovik's* inscription read *Za Zhenyu Lobanova* ('For Evgeniy Lobanov'). The latter had been killed during a ram-attack in 1942 when flying Il-2s with 18th PShAP.

20

Il-2 of 108th GShAP, Crimea, May 1944
Awarded Guards status on 24 August 1943 as a reward for its combat record as 299th ShAP during the Battle of Kursk, this regiment received 42 Il-2s bought by residents of the Zaporozhie region in May 1944. Each one was adorned with the inscription *Polina Osipenko* in honour of a brave female pilot from Zaporozhie who had set several world records pre-war.

21

Il-2-37 of 75th GShAP, Crimea, May-June 1944
Fitted with two NS-37 37 mm cannon housed in fairings under the wings, the Il-2-37 was built in modest numbers in 1943-44 by Factory No 30. Initially seeing service during the Battle of Kursk with 208th ShAP, pilots found that the modified aircraft handled very much like a fully loaded Il-2. However, the heavy weight of the cannon, and its ammunition (50 rounds per gun), increased the Il-2-37's inertia in a dive and made it more difficult to manoeuvre. Excessive recoil from the cannons when they were fired also made aiming difficult, and it was almost impossible to fire the weapons one at a time because they caused the Il-2-37 to yaw violently. As a direct result of these problems, only 75th GShAP, 1st GShAD would end up receiving production-standard Il-2-37s, which it used between the spring and autumn of 1944. Virtually all of these aircraft had been replaced by standard Il-2s come January 1945, the cannon-armed *Shturmoviks* having either been lost in combat or written off due to routine wear and tear associated with frontline operations. 75th GShAP aircraft differed from Il-2s assigned to other regiments of 1st GShAD by having a horizontal white identification bar on their sides and red or yellow propeller spinners.

22

Il-2 of 75th GShAP, Crimea, May-June 1944
This Il-2, armed with standard 23 mm VYa-23 cannon in the wings, served alongside the Il-2-37s that were issued exclusively to 75th GShAP in the spring of 1944. Built by Factory No 18 in Kuybyshev in March-April 1944, it arrived in the frontline on the eve of the battle for the Crimea. Although this machine has the distinctive horizontal white identification bar associated with 75th GShAP, its propeller spinner has not been repainted red or yellow as was often the case with Il-2s assigned to this regiment.

23

Il-2 of 140th GShAP, 2nd Ukrainian Front, summer 1944
Featuring a yellow propeller spinner tip, white fuselage band and rudder tip and a Guards badge just forward of the wing root, this aircraft was assigned to 140th GShAP, 1st GShAK in mid-1944. Seeing plenty of action in support of the large-scale summer offensives in the Ukraine, the Corps to which this unit was assigned received high praise for its combat effectiveness by the commander of 3rd Guards Tank Army, Gen Rybalko. He wrote, 'Attack aircraft pilots from 1st GShAK displayed exceptional bravery on the battlefield during their close cooperation with 3rd Guards Tank Army'.

24

Il-2 of 6th GShAP, 1st Baltic Front, August 1944
Displaying non-standard five-pointed stars, this aircraft was assigned to the very first Il-2 Guards unit in the summer of 1944. 6th GShAP was created from 215th ShAP following the issuing of Order No 352 by the People's Commissar of Defence on 6 December 1941. Having seen near-constant action for three long years, the regiment once again found itself in the thick of things serving with the 1st Baltic Front during the East Prussia operation of August 1944. 6th GShAP operated alongside other Il-2 air units from an airfield on the outskirts of Radvilishkis during this offensive. Engaging the enemy in the towns of Autse, Kruopyay, Yuzefovo and Kelme, regimental pilots especially distinguished themselves during combat operations on the outskirts of Shaulyay. Here, pilots destroyed newly-erected German pontoon bridge crossings that spanned the Venta River and then knocked out a large number of panzers and other vehicles that had broken through to the Shaulyay-Kelme road. Additionally, six Il-2s and six Yak-3s intercepted eight Ju 87s and four Fw 190s, with seven Stukas and a Focke-Wulf fighter being shot down during the ensuing engagement – three of the dive-bombers fell to the Soviet attack aircraft.

25

Il-2 of 6th GShAP, 1st Baltic Front, August 1944
Also adorned with non-standard five-pointed stars, this Il-2 was assigned to 6th GShAP in the summer of 1944 as well.

26

Il-2 of 154th GShAP, 3rd Byelorussian Front, autumn 1944
Assigned to Capt Yury S Afanasiev, this aircraft later the bore the inscription *Za Borisa* ('for Boris') on the left side of its fuselage in honour of his flight leader, Boris Kononov, who was killed in action in the autumn of 1944. Part of 307th ShAD, 3rd ShAK, 154th GShAP had served as 211th ShAP until made a Guards unit with the issuing of Order No 55 by the People's Commissar of Defence on 14 April 1944.

27
Il-2 of 154th GShAP, 3rd Byelorussian Front, autumn 1944
Also assigned to 154th GShAP in the autumn of 1944, this aircraft has a non-standard red tip to its propeller spinner and lacks the red edging on the diagonal white rudder stripe as seen on the aircraft in Profile 26.

28
Il-2 of 154th GShAP, 3rd Byelorussian Front, autumn 1944
When hostilities came to an end in the Minsk sector in mid-1944, 3rd ShAK from the reserve of the Supreme High Command General Headquarters provided support to units of the 3rd Byelorussian Front, which were tasked with liberating Lithuania in August 1944. 154th GShAP, 307th ShAD, 3rd ShAK was deployed to Patsunay airfield, on the Neman River. The regiment, which remained at Patsunay until late August, distinguished itself during the liberation of Kaunas, Shaulyay, and Klaipeda.

29
Il-2 of 6th GShAP, 1st Baltic Front, January 1945
The inscription displayed on this aircraft reads 'To the Hero of Soviet Union Pavlov from the workers of Kustanay town'. Upon its arrival in the frontline, the Il-2 had been presented to Capt I F Pavlov, who was then a squadron leader in 6th GShAP. Under the decree of the USSR Supreme Council Presidium dated 23 February 1945, Capt Pavlov was awarded the title of HSU for the second time. Pavlov subsequently saw action in this aircraft when his regiment targeted enemy forces in East Prussia during the Red Army assault on Königsberg (now Kaliningrad) in April 1945.

30 & 31
Il-2 of 76th GShAP, 1st Baltic Front, January 1945
This aircraft was assigned to legendary Il-2 pilot Capt Musa G Gareev, who had been promoted to flight leader of the 2nd Air Squadron during the Byelorussian operation in July-August 1944. Following additional sorties in the Baltic states, he was appointed navigator of 76th GShAP, while still acting as a flight leader for the 2nd Air Squadron. Nondescript Il-2 'White 24' was Gareev's mount throughout this period, he and his permanent air gunner Sgt Kiryanov taking the fight to the enemy in this aircraft during the liberation of the Crimea and Byelorussia, as well as in East Prussia. The Il-2 was damaged in a dogfight with an Fw 190 in February 1945, and following repairs, it was handed over to another crew. Its final fate is unknown. M G Gareev, who was a stalwart of the Il-2 community, had been promoted to the rank of captain and decorated with the Order of the Red Star and the Order of Alexander Nevsky at the end of hostilities in the Crimea in May 1944 – 1st GShAD command also recommended him for the title of HSU in May and September of that year. Regimental commanding officer D K Bochko finally grounded Gareev on 25 February 1945, by which time he had flown 357 combat sorties.

32
Il-2 of 90th GShAP, 1st Baltic Front, April 1945
This colourful Il-2 was assigned to HSU Capt G T Beregovoy (who later became an cosmonaut) during the final weeks of the war in Europe. 90th GShAP, along with other regiments from 4th GShAD, 5th ShAK, was based at an airfield near the village of Konchani, in Czechoslovakia. Armour and motorised convoys of the *Wehrmacht's* Scherner group, which tried to fight their way through Czechoslovakia in an effort to surrender to US forces, became the last targets attacked by Capt Beregovoy and his comrades-in-arms in April 1945. The breakthrough failed and the Scherner group was destroyed.

INDEX

References to illustrations are shown in **bold**. Plates are shown with page and caption locators in brackets.